WeightWatchers®

COOK SMART desserts

Delicious desserts for everyday and every occasion

SIMON & SCHUSTER
A CBS COMPANY

First published in Great Britain by Simon & Schuster UK Ltd, 2010
A CBS Company

Weight Watchers Publications: Jane Griffiths, Nina McKerlie, Donna Watts and Tori Rozputynski.

Recipes written by: Sue Ashworth, Sue Beveridge, Tamsin Burnett-Hall, Cas Clarke, Siân Davies, Roz Denny, Becky Johnson, Kim Morphew,
Joy Skipper, Penny Stephens and Wendy Veale.

Photography by: Iain Bagwell, Steve Baxter, Steve Lee and Juliet Piddington.
Design and typesetting by Tiger Media Ltd.
Printed and bound in China.

A CIP catalogue for this book is available from the British Library

ISBN 978-0-85720-029-7

1 3 5 7 9 10 8 6 4 2

Pictured on the front cover: Banana and Strawberry Cheesecake p42, Vanilla Mousses with Plums p92, Rich Chocolate Mousse Cake p10,
Sicilian Cassata p116.
Pictured on the back cover: Baked Apple and Blackberry Meringes p66, Pear Tart with Cinnamon Topping p144, Baked Figs with Orange p41,
Easy Chocolate Soufflé p20.
Pictured on the introduction: Chocolate Goo Pudding p18, Raspberry Slice p54, Cherry Batter Pudding p132, Mango Cheesecake Sundae p98.

 POINTS ® value logo: You'll find this easy to read **POINTS** value logo on every recipe throughout this book. The logo represents the number of
POINTS values per serving each recipe contains. Weight Watchers offers you a healthy and sustainable way to lose weight.
For more information about Weight Watchers call 08457 123 000 or visit www.weightwatchers.co.uk

V This symbol denotes a vegetarian recipe and assumes that, where relevant, free range eggs, vegetarian cheese, vegetarian virtually fat free
fromage frais, vegetarian low fat crème fraîche and vegetarian low fat yogurts are used. Virtually fat free fromage frais, low fat crème fraîche and
low fat yogurts may contain traces of gelatine so they are not always vegetarian. Please check the labels.

✱ This symbol denotes a dish that can be frozen.

Recipe notes
Egg size: Medium, unless otherwise stated.
All fruits and vegetables: Medium sized, unless [...]
Raw eggs: Only the freshest eggs should be use[d ...] [av]oid recipes with eggs that are not fully cooked
or raw.
Stock: Stock cubes used in recipes, unless othe[...] [pa]cket instructions.
Recipe timings: These are approximate and mea[...] [ti]me includes all the steps up to and following the
main cooking time(s).
Microwaves: Timings and temperatures are for [...] [yo]ur own microwave.
Low fat spread: Where a recipe states to use a l[...] [le]ss than 38% should be used.

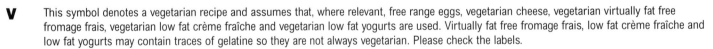

Contents

Introduction

Delicious desserts – this is the ideal book for anyone with a sweet tooth who wants to enjoy healthy versions of their favourite treats and still keep their weight loss on track. From rich chocolate to steamed puddings, this book is full of sweet recipes for finishing off a meal. Impress your friends and family or just treat yourself – there is something here for everyone. Light and fluffy meringues, sweet and fresh fruit, fun jellies and mousses, and much, much more, *Cook Smart Desserts* is a must have for any cook.

About Weight Watchers

For more than 40 years Weight Watchers has been helping people around the world to lose weight using a long term sustainable approach. Weight Watchers successful weight loss system is based on four tried and trusted principles:

- Eating healthily

- Being more active

- Adjusting behaviour to help weight loss

- Getting support in weekly meetings

Our unique **POINTS** system empowers you to manage your food plan and make wise recipe choices for a healthier, happier you.

Basic Ingredients

Milk

Always use skimmed milk, rather than whole or semi-skimmed, unless otherwise stated in the recipe.

Eggs

Always bring eggs to room temperature before using. A cold egg won't whisk well and the shell will crack if placed in hot water.

Fats and Oils

The majority of recipes use low fat cooking spray rather than oil. Low fat cooking spray can be either olive oil or sunflower oil based. Try both and see which you prefer. Generally, low fat spread is used in recipes rather than butter.

Cheese and Yogurt

The cheese used in these recipes is low fat Cheddar, low fat soft cheese or virtually fat free fromage frais. Many recipes use yogurt. Always choose either 0% fat Greek yogurt or low fat natural. All of these products are easy to find in a supermarket.

Chocolate

Use good quality dark chocolate (at least 70% cocoa solids) and the best quality white chocolate you can find for cooking. This means you will get a rich chocolate taste without having to use so much.

Sugar

Many recipes use artificial sweetener as a low calorie replacement for sugar. Where sugar is listed, always try to use the type of sugar suggested as this will affect the flavour.

Dried Fruit

Most dried fruits are ready to eat and don't need soaking, but if the packet is not marked 'ready to eat' you can soak the fruit in a little water first to plump it up if you wish. Always wash and dry glacé cherries.

Planning Ahead

Use the list opposite to keep your store cupboard well stocked with items that can be turned into delicious desserts with the addition of just a few fresh ingredients. Decide what you want to cook before you go shopping, check your store cupboard ingredients and make a list of what you need.

Store Cupboard Suggestions

almonds, flaked

amaretti biscuits

apricots, canned

artificial sweetener

baking powder

bicarbonate of soda

bread, low calorie

cardamom pods

cherries, glacé

chocolate (70% cocoa, milk, white, low fat drink)

cocoa powder, unsweetened

coffee, instant

condensed milk

cornflour

cream of tartar

custard (low fat ready made, powder)

digestive biscuits, reduced fat

elderflower cordial

flour (plain, self raising, wholemeal)

fruit, dried (e.g. tropical mix, apricots, peaches, pears, figs, sultanas, raisins, cranberries)

gelatine

ginger in syrup

golden syrup

honey, runny

jam, reduced sugar (strawberry)

jelly, sugar free (orange, lemon and lime)

lemon curd

low fat cooking spray

lychees, canned

maple syrup

marmalade, low calorie

marshmallows

mint flavouring

mulled wine spice bag

oats (bran, oatmeal, porridge)

oil (vegetable, corn)

orange extract

orange flower water

peaches, canned (slices, halves)

pears, canned (halves)

pineapple, canned (pieces, rings)

pistachio nuts

polenta

prunes, canned

rice, ground

rice cakes (caramel)

spices, ground (mixed, cinnamon, ginger, nutmeg)

sponge fingers

sugar (granulated, caster, golden caster, soft light brown, icing, demerara, light and dark muscovado, fruit/fructose)

treacle

vanilla (extract, pods)

vinegar, balsamic

walnut pieces

Chocolate
Heaven

Everyone loves chocolate, so here are some wickedly wonderful recipes such as Rich Chocolate Mousse Cake, Orange Profiteroles with Chocolate and Orange Sauce, Chocolate Fondue and Chocolate, Pear and Toffee Roulade.

Nothing beats chocolate
for a rich treat

Rich Chocolate Mousse Cake

This is a really rich, mousse-like dessert cake. Made with whisked egg whites, the result is a delicious, moist and intensely chocolatey gâteau. Serve warm, dusted with mixed spice and icing sugar.

Serves 12

125 g (4½ oz) low fat spread

250 g (9 oz) dark chocolate (minimum 70% cocoa solids), broken into pieces

3 eggs, separated

50 g (1¾ oz) golden caster sugar

1½ teaspoons mixed spice

3 egg whites

½ teaspoon icing sugar, for dusting

---

4 POINTS values per serving
45½ POINTS values per recipe

C **199 calories** per serving

Takes **20 minutes** to prepare,
45 minutes to bake + cooling

V

✱ not recommended

1 Preheat the oven to Gas Mark 4/180°C/fan oven 160°C. Line the base of a 20 cm (8 inch) springform cake tin with non stick baking parchment.

2 Melt the low fat spread in a saucepan. Remove from the heat and add the chocolate, stirring to dissolve. If there are any lumps of chocolate left after a minute or so, return to a low heat, continue stirring until dissolved and then remove again from the heat.

3 In a large bowl, whisk the egg yolks with half the caster sugar and 1 teaspoon of the mixed spice until pale and thick. Fold in the chocolate mixture.

4 In a separate, clean, grease-free bowl, whisk all the egg whites until they form stiff peaks. Gradually whisk in the remaining caster sugar until the egg whites are glossy and stiff.

5 Add a large spoonful of the egg whites to the chocolate mixture and fold in quickly to slacken it. Carefully fold in the remaining whites until fully incorporated. Spoon into the prepared tin and bake for 40–45 minutes until risen. Cool in the tin with a piece of foil over the top to soften the crust.

6 To serve, loosen the edges with a round ended knife and remove the springform tin. Carefully slide the cake from the base and lining on to a plate. Mix together the remaining mixed spice and the icing sugar and dust over the cake. Serve warm in wedges.

Tips Don't worry if the cake sinks – it's similar to a soufflé so expect it to.

It's best to enjoy it on the same day you bake it, but it can be refreshed quickly in the microwave the following day.

Chocolate, Pear and Toffee Roulade

A roulade is easy to make but always looks spectacular – perfect for when you have guests.

Serves 6

3 eggs
75 g (2¾ oz) caster sugar
60 g (2 oz) self raising flour, sifted
15 g (½ oz) cocoa powder, sifted
1 pear, cored and diced
250 g (9 oz) low fat toffee yogurt
a kettle full of boiling water
65 g (2½ oz) white or dark chocolate, broken into small pieces

---

4 POINTS values per serving
25 POINTS values per recipe

C 220 calories per serving

Takes **20 minutes** to prepare,
12 minutes to cook + cooling

V

✱ recommended (unfilled)

1 Preheat the oven to Gas Mark 4/180°C/fan oven 160°C. Line a 30 x 20 cm (12 x 8 inch) baking tin with baking parchment and cut another, slightly larger, piece to use later.

2 In a clean, grease-free bowl, whisk the eggs for a minute. Add the sugar and whisk for a further 3 minutes, or until the mixture has doubled in size and resembles whipped cream. (If you don't have an electric beater, this will take 15 minutes with a hand whisk.)

3 Gently fold in the flour and cocoa with a large metal spoon and transfer to the prepared tin. Bake for 10–12 minutes.

4 While still hot, loosen the edges with a knife and turn out on to the other sheet of baking parchment. Peel away the old parchment. Roll up loosely with the new parchment lining the roll, cover with a clean, damp tea towel and leave to cool completely. Meanwhile, mix the pear with the yogurt, saving a little of the yogurt for the topping.

5 Pour boiling water into a bowl or pan and put the chocolate into a heatproof dish. Stand the dish over the pan and leave for 10 minutes to allow the chocolate to melt. Gently unroll the sponge and remove the parchment. Spread the pear mixture over the roulade, then roll it back up.

6 Drizzle the reserved yogurt and melted chocolate over the roulade and trim the ends. Slice into six servings.

Tip You can make the roulade the day before. Simply chill and remove from the fridge an hour before serving to bring to room temperature. This prevents the chocolate from cracking when slicing the roulade.

Hot Chocolate Soufflé with Poached Pears

Try this for a special dessert.

Serves 4

low fat cooking spray
300 ml (10 fl oz) semi skimmed milk
50 g (1¾ oz) dark chocolate (minimum 70% cocoa solids), broken into pieces
25 g (1 oz) butter
15 g (½ oz) plain flour
25 g (1 oz) cornflour
25 g (1 oz) caster sugar
a few drops of vanilla extract
2 large eggs, separated

For the pears

25 g (1 oz) caster sugar
2 teaspoons lemon juice
2 ripe Comice pears, peeled, cored and each half sliced into 4 wedges

---

6 POINTS values per serving
24½ POINTS values per recipe

C **310 calories** per serving

Takes **25 minutes** to prepare,
30 minutes to cook

V

✱ not recommended

1 Lightly spray a 20 cm (8 inch) soufflé dish with the cooking spray.

2 For the pears, put 150 ml (5 fl oz) of water, the sugar and lemon juice in a lidded saucepan, add the pears, cover and gently poach for 12–15 minutes, or until completely translucent. Remove from the heat and set aside.

3 Meanwhile, make the soufflé. In a small saucepan gently heat half the milk with the chocolate, stirring constantly. When the chocolate has melted, remove from the heat and stir in the remaining milk.

4 Melt the butter in another saucepan, add the flour and cornflour and quickly blend in the chocolate milk. Bring to the boil, stirring constantly, and cook for 1 minute. Remove from the heat and stir in the sugar and vanilla extract.

5 In a clean, grease-free bowl, whisk the egg whites until they form soft peaks. Beat the egg yolks into the chocolate mixture, then fold in the egg whites. Pour the mixture into the soufflé dish and cover with a piece of thick kitchen foil, tying securely with string.

6 Steam over a pan of boiling water for 30 minutes or until just firm to touch.

7 Serve the soufflé with the pear wedges and a little of the poaching juice.

Tip To steam, bring a pan of water to the boil and place the soufflé dish in a steamer on top, making sure the water level is below the steamer. Steam for the required time, topping up with boiling water if necessary.

White Chocolate Mocha Creams

This is a simple-to-make, pretty, swirled, mousse-like dessert that is great after dinner with coffee.

Serves 4

200 g (7 oz) virtually fat free natural fromage frais
25 g (1 oz) icing sugar
1 tablespoon instant coffee, dissolved in 2 tablespoons boiling water
50 g (1¾ oz) white chocolate, broken into pieces
100 g (3½ oz) Quark cheese
100 g (3½ oz) ricotta cheese
cocoa powder, for dusting

 4 POINTS values per serving
15 POINTS values per recipe

C **180 calories** per serving

Takes **15 minutes** + minimum **30 minutes** chilling

V

✻ not recommended

1 In a bowl, mix together the fromage frais, sugar and coffee until smooth. Set aside.

2 Place the chocolate pieces into a heatproof bowl and set over a pan of simmering water, making sure the water does not touch the bottom of the bowl. Melt the chocolate, stirring occasionally, then remove from the heat.

3 In a separate bowl, beat together the Quark, ricotta and chocolate until smooth.

4 Stir the two mixtures together lightly to give a swirly pattern, then spoon into serving glasses. Chill for at least 30 minutes before serving with a dusting of cocoa powder.

Tip For the best results, use the best quality white chocolate you can find.

Orange Profiteroles with Chocolate and Orange Sauce

Choux pastry is light and crisp and easy to make. Fill the profiteroles with orange flavoured sweetened ricotta cheese.

Makes 18 (Serves 6)

60 g (2 oz) plain flour
40 g (1½ oz) low fat spread
1 egg
1 egg white

For the filling
150 g (5½ oz) ricotta cheese
2 teaspoons finely grated orange zest
1 tablespoon icing sugar, sifted

For the chocolate and orange sauce
100 g (3½ oz) dark chocolate (minimum 70% cocoa solids), broken into pieces
200 ml (7 fl oz) skimmed milk
1 tablespoon golden syrup
finely grated zest of an orange

 5 POINTS values per serving
29 POINTS values per recipe

C **234 calories** per serving

🕐 Takes **25 minutes** to prepare,
25 minutes to bake

V

✳ not recommended

1 Preheat the oven to Gas Mark 6/200°C/fan oven 180°C. Line two baking trays with non stick baking parchment. Sift the flour on to a plate.

2 Place the low fat spread in a large pan with 125 ml (4 fl oz) of water. Bring to the boil then remove from the heat. Add the flour and beat thoroughly until the mixture is smooth and forms a ball.

3 Whisk together the egg and egg white and then gradually beat the eggs into the flour mixture. Make sure the mixture is beaten well to incorporate the air that makes the buns rise.

4 Use a teaspoon to place 18 dollops of the mixture on the baking trays, leaving room for them to expand.

5 Bake for 20 minutes until golden. Do not open the oven door during this time or the profiteroles will sink. Remove from the oven and pierce each one with a skewer to let out the steam. Return to the oven for 5 minutes to dry out. Transfer to a wire rack to cool.

6 Meanwhile, make the chocolate and orange sauce. Chop the chocolate pieces into smaller pieces. Warm the milk in a small pan to just below boiling, then remove from the heat. Add the chocolate and stir to dissolve, reheating very gently if necessary. Stir in the golden syrup and orange zest.

7 To fill the profiteroles, mix the filling ingredients together, then carefully slit the buns and spoon or pipe in the mixture. Serve three each, with the sauce.

Tip Do not fill the buns more than 2 hours before serving otherwise they will go soggy. Try to make the buns fresh that day.

Chocolate Goo Pudding

Expect a fabulous taste sensation with this gooey pudding.

Serves 6

100 g (3½ oz) dark chocolate (minimum 70% cocoa solids), broken into pieces
2 heaped tablespoons runny honey
2 heaped teaspoons cocoa powder
2 level teaspoons cornflour
2 teaspoons icing sugar, for dusting

For the topping
2 large eggs
60 g (2 oz) muscovado sugar
2 heaped teaspoons cocoa powder

 4½ POINTS values per serving
25½ POINTS values per recipe

C **212 calories** per serving

Takes **20 minutes** to prepare,
10 minutes to cook

V

✱ not recommended

1 Preheat the oven to Gas Mark 5/190°C/fan oven 170°C.

2 In a small saucepan, gently heat the chocolate pieces, honey, 2 teaspoons of the cocoa powder, cornflour and 200 ml (7 fl oz) of water, stirring constantly, until the sauce is thick and smooth.

3 Divide the sauce between six ramekins or heatproof glasses.

4 In a large bowl whisk the eggs and sugar together until pale, thick and very airy. This will take 4–5 minutes. Sift in the remaining 2 teaspoons of cocoa powder and fold in using a large metal spoon, so that the air is not lost.

5 Share the topping between the ramekins. Stand them on a baking tray and bake for 8–10 minutes.

6 Remove from the oven, sprinkle with icing sugar and serve immediately.

Variations Use light soft brown sugar instead of muscovado, if you prefer. The **POINTS** values will remain the same.

You can use golden syrup instead of honey, for the same **POINTS** values per serving.

Easy Chocolate Soufflé

If you avoid soufflés because timing the preparation and cooking is so difficult, you'll love these.
Cook them in advance and when you're ready to eat dessert just pop them back into the oven – they fluff
up beautifully.

Serves 2

low fat cooking spray
**25 g (1 oz) dark chocolate (minimum 70% cocoa
  solids), broken into pieces**
1½ tablespoons Amaretto liqueur
2 eggs, separated
40 g (1½ oz) caster sugar
1 heaped teaspoon plain flour
½ teaspoon icing sugar, for dusting

5 *POINTS* values per serving
9½ *POINTS* values per recipe

C **285 calories** per serving

Takes **10 minutes** to prepare,
22 minutes to cook + cooling

V

✻ not recommended

1 Preheat the oven to Gas Mark 5/190°C/fan oven 170°C. Spray two large ramekins (200 ml/7 fl oz) with the cooking spray.

2 In a small microwave proof bowl, melt the chocolate in the microwave by heating on High for a few seconds. (If you don't have a microwave, you can melt the chocolate in a small heatproof bowl placed over a small saucepan of simmering water, making sure the water does not touch the bottom of the bowl.) Briskly stir in the liqueur until you have a smooth consistency, then add the egg yolks, caster sugar and flour.

3 In a clean, grease-free bowl, whisk the egg whites until they form stiff peaks.

4 Fold the chocolate mixture into the egg whites with a metal spoon and divide between the prepared ramekin dishes. Bake for 10–12 minutes until just starting to set and then remove from the oven and put to one side to cool.

5 About 30 minutes before you want to serve the soufflés, preheat the oven to Gas Mark 6/200°C/fan oven 180°C. Pop the soufflés back into the oven and bake for a further 10 minutes until they puff up.

6 To serve, place the ramekins on two small plates and lightly dust with the icing sugar.

Tip To dust with icing sugar, hold a tea strainer over the soufflés, gently spoon the icing sugar into the strainer and shake lightly over each one in turn.

Variation If you like you can use other spirits such as Tia Maria, rum or brandy instead of Amaretto. The ***POINTS*** values per serving will remain the same.

Choc-orange Pancakes

This recipe will satisfy not only your sweet tooth but your chocolate cravings too.

Serves 4

100 g (3½ oz) plain flour
15 g (½ oz) cocoa powder
2 teaspoons golden syrup
1 large egg
300 ml (10 fl oz) skimmed milk
finely grated zest of an orange
2–3 drops orange extract (optional)
2 tablespoons artificial sweetener, to taste
2 teaspoons vegetable or sunflower oil

---

3 POINTS values per serving
11 POINTS values per recipe

C   **180 calories** per serving

Takes **5 minutes** to prepare,
45 minutes to cook + **1 hour** standing time

V

✻   not recommended

1 Sift the flour and cocoa powder into a bowl. Add the golden syrup, egg and milk, and whisk thoroughly to mix.

2 Add the orange zest and orange extract, if using, with the sweetener. Leave the mixture to stand in a cool place for 1 hour.

3 When ready to cook, heat a non stick frying pan over a medium heat with a couple of drops of the oil. When the oil is hot, ladle about 4 tablespoons of the mixture into the pan. Tilt the pan to spread the mixture evenly over the surface.

4 After 2–3 minutes, when the pancake lifts easily at the sides, flip it over with a palette knife or fish slice.

5 Cook for a further 2–3 minutes, and then turn the pancake out on to a plate. Keep it warm while you cook the others. The recipe makes eight pancakes; serve two each.

Tip Orange extract can be found in supermarkets alongside the cake colourings and flavourings.

Variations For a special occasion, mix 200 g (7 oz) 0% fat Greek yogurt with sweetener and a little Cointreau. Divide the mixture between the four portions of pancakes, for an extra ½ **POINTS** value per serving.

To make apple pancakes, make as above substituting a teaspoon of cinnamon for the cocoa and omitting the orange zest and and extract. Grate one apple and add a teaspoon of the grated apple once the pancake mixture is in the pan, and before it is flipped. Add a little cinnamon to the apple if you like. The **POINTS** values will be 2½ per serving.

Chocolate Rice Pudding

A good pud for a wintry night. This low **POINTS** value comfort food can be ready in 15 minutes.

Serves 4

40 g (1½ oz) ground rice
2 tablespoons cocoa powder
2 tablespoons artificial sweetener
600 ml (20 fl oz) skimmed milk

1½ POINTS values per serving
5½ POINTS values per recipe

C **120 calories** per serving

Takes **15 minutes**

V

✳ not recommended

1 Place the ground rice, cocoa powder and sweetener in a small, non stick saucepan and stir together. Add a little milk and stir to a paste, then gradually add the rest of the milk to make a smooth blend.

2 Bring to the boil and simmer for 10 minutes, stirring occasionally. Serve immediately.

Tip This can be made with two 22 g sachets of low calorie hot chocolate powder instead of the sweetener and cocoa powder. The **POINTS** values will remain the same.

Wicked Chocolate Cake

A light but richly flavoured cake that will sink a little when it comes out of the oven. Serve with a 60 g (2 oz) scoop of low fat vanilla ice cream per person, for an extra 1 **POINTS** value per serving.

Serves 10

50 g (1¾ oz) dark chocolate (minimun 70% cocoa solids), broken into pieces

50 g (1¾ oz) low fat spread

1 tablespoon cocoa powder

3 eggs, separated

5 tablespoons artificial sweetener

75 g (2¾ oz) self raising flour, sifted

1 teaspoon icing sugar, for dusting

---

2 POINTS values per serving
18½ POINTS values per recipe

108 calories per serving

Takes **20 minutes** to prepare,
35 minutes to cook + cooling

V

✱ recommended

1 Preheat the oven to Gas Mark 3/160°C/fan oven 140°C and line a 20 cm (8 inch) cake tin with baking parchment.

2 Put the chocolate into a bowl with the low fat spread, cocoa powder and 50 ml (2 fl oz) of cold water. Set over a saucepan of barely simmering water until melted. Remove from the heat and stir together.

3 In a clean, grease-free bowl, whisk the egg whites until they form stiff peaks. In a seperate bowl, whisk the sweetener and egg yolks together until pale and creamy.

4 Add the chocolate mixture to the egg yolk mix and whisk together. Fold in the flour and lastly the egg whites with a large metal spoon.

5 Pour into the prepared baking tin and bake for 35 minutes until the cake is springy to the touch and a skewer inserted in the middle comes out clean. Cool in the tin for 10 minutes before turning out.

6 When cool, dust with the icing sugar to serve.

Chocolate Orange Tiramisu

Try this Italian classic dessert with a slight twist. Bon appétit.

Serves 4

2 teaspoons instant coffee, dissolved in 100 ml (3½ fl oz) hot water, cooled

2 tablespoons Amaretto, Grand Marnier or Cointreau liqueur

200 g (7 oz) low fat soft cheese

200 g (7 oz) low fat natural fromage frais

½ teaspoon vanilla extract

1 teaspoon finely grated orange zest, plus 4 fine orange zest shreds, to decorate

2 heaped teaspoons cocoa powder

1 tablespoon artificial sweetener

12 sponge fingers, halved

1 In a shallow bowl, mix together the cooled coffee with the Amaretto, Grand Marnier or Cointreau.

2 In another bowl, beat together the soft cheese, fromage frais, vanilla extract, orange zest, 1 teaspoon of the cocoa powder and the sweetener until smooth.

3 To assemble the desserts, line up four medium serving glasses or ramekin dishes. Dip the sponge fingers briefly into the coffee mixture, then layer half of them in the base of the glasses or ramekin dishes as you go along. Top with half the soft cheese mixture. Repeat the layers. Cover and chill the desserts until required.

4 To serve, sprinkle with the remaining cocoa powder and shreds of orange zest.

3½ POINTS values per serving
15 POINTS values per recipe

217 calories per serving

Takes **20 minutes** to prepare

V

✳ recommended

Chocolate Fudge

A little indulgence is good for you, so have a treat with these little squares of chocolate fudge.

Makes 36 squares

low fat cooking spray
175 g (6 oz) golden caster sugar
170 g can evaporated milk
25 g (1 oz) butter

350 g (12 oz) dark chocolate
(minimum 70% cocoa solids),
broken into pieces
100 g (3½ oz) white
marshmallows

1 Spray an 18 cm (7 inch) square cake tin with the cooking spray.

2 In a large, heavy-based saucepan, add the sugar, evaporated milk and butter and bring up to the boil, stirring constantly. Reduce the heat to medium and boil gently for 4 minutes, stirring all the time.

3 Add the chocolate and marshmallows to the saucepan. Remove from the heat and stir until smooth.

4 Pour into the prepared tin and leave until cold. Refrigerate until firm – about 2 hours. Cut into 36 squares.

2 POINTS values per serving
68 POINTS values per recipe

C **100 calories** per serving

Takes **15 minutes** to prepare,
10 minutes to cook + **2 hours** chilling

V

✱ not recommended

Tip Store the fudge in the fridge to keep its firm texture.

Chocolate Bread Pudding with Luscious Chocolate Sauce

Chocolate pudding doesn't have to be high in **POINTS** values, it just needs to be delicious.

Serves 4

low fat cooking spray
6 slices Weight Watchers white bread, crusts removed
600 ml (20 fl oz) skimmed milk
2 tablespoons unsweetened cocoa powder
2 eggs
25 g (1 oz) dark or light muscovado sugar
1 teaspoon vanilla extract
1 teaspoon icing sugar, for dusting

For the sauce

25 g (1 oz) dark chocolate (minimum 70% cocoa solids), broken into pieces
1 tablespoon unsweetened cocoa powder
150 ml (5 fl oz) skimmed milk
1 tablespoon cornflour
artificial sweetener, to taste

 4½ POINTS values per serving
18½ POINTS values per recipe

C **271 calories** per serving

Takes **20 minutes** to prepare,
40 minutes to cook + **1–2 hours** soaking

V

✱ not recommended

1 Spray a 20 cm (8 inch) square baking dish with the cooking spray. Cut the bread into squares and layer them in the baking dish.

2 In a pan, heat the milk and cocoa powder until lukewarm, stirring occasionally. Whisk the eggs, sugar and vanilla extract together. Add the warm milk mixture and beat well. Using a sieve, strain into the baking dish, making sure that all the bread is covered. Cover and chill for 1–2 hours.

3 Preheat the oven to Gas Mark 4/180°C/fan oven 160°C. Bake the pudding until set, about 35–40 minutes. When cooked, allow to stand for 5 minutes whilst making the sauce.

4 To make the sauce, put the chocolate, cocoa powder, milk and cornflour into a saucepan. Heat gently, stirring until smooth and blended. Add sweetener, to taste.

5 Sprinkle the pudding with icing sugar and serve immediately with the chocolate sauce.

Variation Instead of serving the pudding with the chocolate sauce, try it with 1 tablespoon of low fat natural fromage frais per person. This will reduce the **POINTS** values to 4 per serving.

Blueberry Chocolate Cups

Elegant plain chocolate cups that can be filled with any number of alternatives. Here blueberries and a blackberry yogurt have been used – a combination that is sure to tempt your tastebuds.

Serves 4

50 g (1¾ oz) white chocolate, broken into pieces
2 x 120 g pots low fat blackberry yogurts
100 g (3½ oz) fresh blueberries

2 POINTS values per serving
9 POINTS values per recipe

C **110 calories** per serving

Takes **20 minutes** + at least **30 minutes** chilling

V

✱ not recommended

1 Melt the chocolate in a bowl over simmering water then brush it over the insides of four paper cup cases using a pastry brush. Place each cup into a different section of a Yorkshire pudding tin and refrigerate until set. Repeat, building up layers of chocolate in the paper cases until you have used all the chocolate.

2 When the chocolate has set, very carefully peel the paper away and place the cups on a serving plate.

3 Fill the cups with yogurt then top with the blueberries and serve, or chill until serving.

Tips It is quick and easy to melt cooking chocolate in the microwave. Just break it up into a glass or plastic bowl and put it on High for about 30 seconds. Stir and use or, if not quite melted, heat in the microwave on High for another 10 seconds, and so on until melted.

When handling chocolate, try to keep your hands as cool as possible or wear cotton gloves, if you have any.

If you have the time, also brush a few small leaves, like fresh bay leaves, with the melted chocolate on their top side. When the chocolate has set, peel the leaf away and use the chocolate leaves as decorations for your desserts.

Variation If blueberries are not in season, they may be very expensive so substitute with plums and very low fat vanilla yogurt, or tangerine segments and virtually fat free strawberry yogurt, for the same **POINTS** values per serving.

White Choc Chip Brownies

Who doesn't love a good brownie? Stored in an airtight container, these chocolate delights will be even more gooey and fudgey the day after baking.

Makes 12

low fat cooking spray
175 g (6 oz) self raising flour
40 g (1½ oz) cocoa powder
a pinch of salt
100 g (3½ oz) light muscovado sugar
1 egg, beaten
1 teaspoon vanilla extract
100 g (3½ oz) low fat natural yogurt
80 g (3 oz) low fat spread, melted
25 g (1 oz) white chocolate chips

2½ *POINTS* values per serving
29½ *POINTS* values per recipe

139 **calories** per serving

Takes **10 minutes** to prepare,
20 minutes to cook + cooling

V

✱ recommended

1 Preheat the oven to Gas Mark 4/180°C/fan oven 160°C.

2 Lightly spray a 20 cm (8 inch) square cake tin with the cooking spray and line it with baking parchment. Sift the flour, cocoa powder and the pinch of salt into a mixing bowl and stir in the sugar.

3 Whisk the egg, vanilla extract and yogurt together with 150 ml (5 fl oz) of cold water. Pour into the dry ingredients, add the melted spread and mix well until smooth. Stir in the chocolate chips, then pour the batter into the lined tin.

4 Bake for 20 minutes until set and the top is slightly cracked. The brownies should still be slightly sticky in the centre. Cool in the tin and cut into 12 pieces. Store in an airtight container.

Chocolate Puddings with Chocolate Sauce

Delicious little chocolate puddings that are sure to please.

Serves 4

low fat cooking spray
2 eggs
50 g (1¾ oz) caster sugar
75 g (2¾ oz) plain flour
25 g (1 oz) cocoa powder
2 drops vanilla extract
1 tablespoon skimmed milk

For the sauce
1 sachet low fat chocolate drink
300 ml (10 fl oz) skimmed milk
1 tablespoon cornflour

3½ **POINTS** values per serving
14 **POINTS** values per recipe

C **220 calories** per serving

Takes **25 minutes** to prepare,
15 minutes to bake + **20 minutes** cooling

V

✱ not recommended

1 Lightly spray four individual ramekin dishes or dariole moulds with the cooking spray and line the base of each with a circle of non stick baking parchment. Preheat the oven to Gas Mark 4/180°C/fan oven 160°C.

2 To make the sauce, place the sachet of chocolate in a medium saucepan with the milk and cornflour. Cook, whisking, until the sauce is slightly thickened. Remove the pan from the heat and allow the mixture to cool for about 20 minutes.

3 Place the eggs and caster sugar in a mixing bowl and whisk until the mixture becomes fluffy and pale in colour.

4 Sift the flour and cocoa powder into the egg mixture, folding it in with a metal spoon along with the vanilla extract and milk. Divide the pudding mixture between the lined ramekin dishes or dariole moulds. Bake for 15 minutes, until the sponges are firm and springy to the touch.

5 Run a round bladed knife around the edge of each pudding. Turn them out on to four serving plates. Drizzle the chocolate sauce over the puddings. Serve them warm.

Variation Fold some finely grated orange zest into the pudding mixture in step 3, to add a citrus tang. The **POINTS** values will remain the same.

Frozen Chocolate Oranges

A creamy, chocolate-orange mousse frozen in an orange shell.

Serves 6

6 oranges

100 g (3½ oz) dark chocolate (minimum 70% cocoa solids), broken into pieces

1 tablespoon cocoa powder, plus extra for dusting

1 teaspoon instant coffee, dissolved in 1 tablespoon boiling water

3 egg whites

50 g (1¾ oz) caster sugar

3½ *POINTS* values per serving
19½ *POINTS* values per recipe

C **190 calories** per serving

Takes **30 minutes** + at least **2 hours** freezing

V

✱ recommended

1 Remove the tops from the oranges and reserve. Scoop out the flesh and discard the pith, reserving the orange shells. Chop the flesh and set aside.

2 Put the chocolate into a heatproof bowl and set over a pan of simmering water until melted (making sure that the water does not touch the bottom of the bowl). Meanwhile, mix the cocoa powder with the coffee paste then stir into the chocolate.

3 In a clean, grease-free bowl, whisk the egg whites until they form stiff peaks then gradually whisk in the sugar. Fold in the chocolate mixture until thoroughly blended then add the chopped orange.

4 Spoon into the orange shells, replace the lids but do not push down, and freeze until firm. Serve dusted with cocoa powder.

Tip These oranges will keep in the freezer for up to 10 days.

Chocolate Fondue

This clever chocolate fondue sauce is rich and indulgent, but surprisingly low in *POINTS* values.

Serves 4

25 g (1 oz) cocoa powder
170 g can evaporated milk
25 g (1 oz) milk chocolate, broken into pieces
2 bananas, sliced
3 clementines or satsumas, segmented
200 g (7 oz) strawberries, hulled

4 *POINTS* values per serving
15½ *POINTS* values per recipe

C **207 calories** per serving

Takes **10 minutes**

V

✳ not recommended

1 Place the cocoa in a non stick saucepan and gradually stir in the evaporated milk to make a smooth sauce.

2 Add the chocolate and place the pan over a medium heat. Bring to a simmer, stirring, then cook for 1 minute until thickened.

3 Pour into small individual bowls and serve with the fruit, to dip into the chocolate fondue sauce.

Fabulous Fruit

Fruit is so versatile – try something unusual like Baked Cardamom and Orange Custards, delicious hot baked fruit such as Baked Peaches, or cold fruit salads like Strawberry Salad or Melon Salad.

Make the most of seasonal fruit
with these great ideas

Baked Peaches

A simple dessert that is perfect for a quick weekday supper.

Serves 4

4 ripe peaches, halved and stoned
4 tablespoons white wine
finely grated zest and juice of ½ an orange
1 tablespoon light brown sugar
2 teaspoons low fat spread
15 g (½ oz) amaretti biscuits, crushed
4 tablespoons half fat crème fraîche, to serve

3 POINTS values per serving
11 POINTS values per recipe

145 calories per serving

Takes **10 minutes** to prepare,
30 minutes to cook

V

✳ not recommended

1 Preheat the oven to Gas Mark 6/200°C/fan oven 180°C.

2 Put the peach halves in an ovenproof dish, cut side up.

3 In a small jug, mix together the wine, orange zest and juice.

4 Pour over the peaches and sprinkle with the sugar. Dot with the low fat spread and bake in the oven for 25–30 minutes until golden and the juices have thickened.

5 Sprinkle over the crushed biscuits and serve with the crème fraîche.

Gooseberry Strudel

Serves 4

400 g (14 oz) gooseberries

finely grated zest of ½ a lemon

2 tablespoons artificial sweetener, plus extra for dusting

30 g (1¼ oz) fresh white breadcumbs

a large pinch of mixed spice, plus extra for dusting

6 sheets of filo pastry (approximately 85 g/3 oz in total, measuring 17 x 32 cm)

low fat cooking spray

1 Preheat the grill to a high heat and preheat the oven to Gas Mark 6/200°C/fan oven 180°C. Put the gooseberries in a saucepan with 2 tablespoons of water, the lemon zest and the sweetener. Bring to a gentle simmer and cook for 5 minutes or until the fruit is soft. Use a little extra sweetener if required.

2 Meanwhile, lay the breadcrumbs on a baking sheet and toast them under the grill for a minute or two until golden and crisp. Sprinkle a good pinch of mixed spice over the top and put to one side.

3 Lay a sheet of filo pastry on your work surface and spray it with the cooking spray. Lay another sheet with the long sides overlapping by about 2.5 cm (1 inch) so the two pieces together form a rough square. Spray again and lay a third sheet on top of the first. Repeat the process until you have used six sheets.

4 Spread the breadcrumbs in a 10 cm (4 inch) band along the bottom edge of the filo pastry, parallel to the join. Leave a gap of pastry about 2.5 cm (1 inch) around the breadcrumbs. Top the breadcrumbs with the gooseberries. Fold in the sides and then roll up loosely from the bottom. Transfer to a baking sheet with the join underneath.

5 Spray the strudel with the cooking spray and bake in the oven for 25 minutes. Serve warm, dusted with sweetener and mixed spice.

1½ *POINTS* values per serving
6 *POINTS* values per recipe

136 **calories** per serving

Takes **30 minutes** to prepare, **25 minutes** to cook

V

* recommended

Baked Figs with Orange

Blood oranges are usually available during the winter months, but if you cannot find them just use regular oranges.

Serves 4

8 ripe figs, quartered

4 oranges, preferably blood oranges, 2 cut into segments and 2 zested and juiced

2 teaspoons artificial sweetener

To serve

1 teaspoon orange flower water

4 tablespoons low fat natural yogurt

1 Preheat the oven to Gas Mark 4/180°C/fan oven 160°C and arrange the fig quarters in an ovenproof dish.

2 Scatter over the orange segments, orange zest and sweetener and drizzle with the orange juice.

3 Bake for 15 minutes or until sticky. Serve drizzled with orange flower water with 1 tablespoon of yogurt per serving.

 1½ POINTS values per serving
6½ POINTS values per recipe

C **113 calories** per serving

Takes **5 minutes** to prepare, **15 minutes** to cook

V

✳ not recommended

Banana and Strawberry Cheesecake

This is a great pudding to share – creamy cheesecake and fresh fruit.

Serves 10

100 g (3½ oz) caramel rice cakes
4 bananas
finely grated zest and juice of 2 lemons
600 g (1 lb 5 oz) low fat soft cheese
1½ tablespoons artificial sweetener
3 tablespoons low fat natural fromage frais
6 eggs, beaten
500 g (1 lb 2 oz) strawberries, hulled and sliced,
  to decorate

4 POINTS values per serving
39 POINTS values per recipe

226 calories per serving

Takes **20 minutes** to prepare,
1½ hours to cook + cooling

V

✱ not recommended

1 Preheat the oven to Gas Mark 2/150°C/fan oven 130°C.

2 Place the rice cakes in a food processor and whizz until crumbly. Mash the bananas with the lemon juice and mix in the rice cake crumbs. Press the mixture into the base of a 23 cm (9 inch) loose bottomed tin.

3 Blend the soft cheese, sweetener and fromage frais together until smooth. Add the eggs and lemon zest and blend again to mix thoroughly.

4 Pour the soft cheese mixture over the base and bake in the oven for 1–1½ hours until set. Leave to cool in the tin.

5 Remove from the tin and decorate with strawberry slices before serving.

Blackberry and Apple Filo Pies

These little crisp pastries filled with juicy fruits are a delicious after dinner low **POINTS** value treat.

Serves 6

350 g (12 oz) cooking apples, peeled, cored and diced
15 g (½ oz) artificial sweetener
a pinch of ground nutmeg
225 g (8 oz) blackberries
1 tablespoon cornflour
6 x 15 g sheets filo pastry
low fat cooking spray

1 Line a baking tray with non stick baking parchment.

2 Place the apples in a small, lidded saucepan with 3 tablespoons of water, the sweetener and nutmeg. Cover and simmer gently for 5 minutes until the apples begin to soften.

3 Stir in the blackberries, cover and cook for a further 2 minutes. Mix the cornflour with 2 tablespoons of cold water and stir into the fruit. Cook, stirring, until the mixture thickens. Remove the pan from the heat and allow to cool.

4 Preheat the oven to Gas Mark 5/190°C/fan oven 170°C. Spray a filo pastry sheet with the cooking spray and fold it in half. Spoon some of the cooled apple and blackberry mixture into the centre of the folded sheet. Now gather up the edges of the pastry and twist them, to seal it like a purse. Place on the baking tray, repeat the process with the remaining pastry sheets and then spray the pastry purses with the cooking spray.

5 Bake for 12–15 minutes, until the pastry is golden and crisp.

1 POINTS value per serving
7 POINTS values per recipe

158 calories per serving

Takes **30 minutes** to prepare,
15 minutes to bake

V

* recommended

Melon Salad

This is an easy dessert that is perfect anytime but delicious during the hot summer months.

Serves 2

2 tablespoons syrup from a jar of ginger

25 g packet fresh mint leaves, stalks removed

100 g (3½ oz) cantaloupe melon, peeled, deseeded and sliced into wedges

100 g (3½ oz) honeydew melon, peeled, deseeded and sliced into wedges

100 g (3½ oz) galia melon, peeled, deseeded and sliced into wedges

To decorate

15 g (½ oz) nugget of ginger in syrup, chopped

a few fresh mint sprigs

1 Bring 150 ml (5 fl oz) of water to the boil in a small saucepan and then add the ginger syrup. Boil rapidly for 10 minutes. Add the mint leaves and set aside for 30 minutes.

2 Pass the syrup through a sieve into a jug, pressing the mint leaves to squeeze out the juices. Put all the melon wedges into a large bowl and pour over the mint infusion. Leave for 15 minutes.

3 Divide the melons and mint infusion between two bowls, scatter over the ginger and mint sprigs and serve.

2 POINTS values per serving
3½ POINTS values per recipe

C **100 calories** per serving

Takes **30 minutes** + **45 minutes** cooling

V

* not recommended

Baked Cardamom and Orange Custards

These easy custards make a superb dinner party dessert.

Serves 4

low fat cooking spray
200 ml (7 fl oz) skimmed milk
4 cardamom pods
2 eggs, beaten
2 tablespoons artificial sweetener
2 oranges

1 *POINTS* value per serving
4½ *POINTS* values per recipe

98 calories per serving

Takes **10 minutes** to prepare,
40 minutes to bake + chilling

V

✳ not recommended

1 Preheat the oven to Gas Mark 3/160°C/fan oven 140°C. Lightly coat four 150 ml (5 fl oz) ovenproof ramekins with the cooking spray.

2 Place the milk in a pan, add the seeds from the cardamom pods and gently warm until hand hot. Remove from the heat and whisk in the eggs and sweetener. Pour the mixture into the prepared ramekins, straining it through a sieve to remove any unmixed egg and the cardamom seeds.

3 Finely grate the zest from 1 orange and stir a little into each ramekin.

4 Place the ramekins in a deep roasting tin and fill with sufficient hot water to come halfway up the sides of the pots. Bake for 40 minutes until just set (they will still wobble slightly). Remove from the oven, allow to cool and then chill.

5 Use a serrated knife to slice the skin from the oranges. Segment the oranges, collecting any juice.

6 To serve, top the custards with the orange segments and juice.

Tip If you prefer, you can serve these custards warm.

Rhubarb Fool

The white chocolate in this creamy, fruit dessert adds a touch of luxury.

Serves 4

500 g (1 lb 2 oz) fresh rhubarb
2 tablespoons fruit sugar (fructose)
60 g (2 oz) white chocolate, broken into pieces
150 ml (5 fl oz) ready to serve low fat custard

1 Place the rhubarb in a medium saucepan with 3 tablespoons of water and the fruit sugar. Bring to a gentle simmer. Continue to simmer for 12–15 minutes until the rhubarb is soft. Take the pan off the heat and leave to cool.

2 Meanwhile, melt the chocolate in a large, heatproof bowl over a saucepan of barely simmering water, making sure the water does not touch the bottom of the bowl. Remove the bowl from the heat.

3 Beat the custard into the melted chocolate.

4 Gently stir the rhubarb into the custard mixture, not combining it completely.

5 Spoon the fool into glasses or individual dishes and chill in the fridge for at least 30 minutes until ready to serve.

2½ **POINTS** values per serving
10½ **POINTS** values per recipe

150 calories per serving

Takes **20 minutes** to prepare,
15 minutes to cook + **30 minutes** chilling

V

✻ not recommended

Tip Rhubarb does vary a lot in sweetness – taste the cooked rhubarb before adding the custard to check whether it is sweet enough. If not, try adding a little more fruit sugar, remembering to adjust the **POINTS** values accordingly. Remember it will become sweeter when combined with the custard and white chocolate.

Apple Pancakes

These little pancake stacks are delicious served with 1 tablespoon of very low fat natural fromage frais or 0% fat Greek yogurt, for an extra ½ *POINTS* value per serving.

Serves 4

2 tablespoons caster sugar	**1 egg**
1 teaspoon ground cinnamon	**125 ml (4 fl oz) skimmed milk**
110 g (4 oz) self raising flour	**2 eating apples**
a pinch of salt	**low fat cooking spray**

1 Mix the sugar and cinnamon together, reserving 2 teaspoons for sprinkling at the end, then place the remainder in a mixing bowl.

2 Sift in the flour and the pinch of salt. Make a well in the centre then break in the egg. Gradually whisk in the milk to give a smooth batter. Peel one of the apples and coarsely grate it into the batter, discarding the core.

3 Lightly coat a non stick frying pan with the cooking spray, then drop in 4 separate tablespoons of batter. Cook for 1½ minutes until browned underneath and bubbly on top, then flip over and cook for 1 minute on the other side. Keep warm and repeat to make a total of 12 pancakes. Core and thinly slice the remaining apple.

4 To serve, layer three pancakes per serving with a quarter of the sliced apple, sprinkling with the cinnamon sugar as you go.

2½ *POINTS* values per serving
10 *POINTS* values per recipe

185 calories per serving

Takes **15 minutes**

V

✱ recommended (pancakes only)

Iced Tropical Grill

A delicious combination of hot and cold, this is sure to get people talking.

Serves 4

1 large ripe pineapple, peeled and sliced into 8 (core removed if preferred)
2 cardamom pods, crushed and husks removed
2 teaspoons artificial sweetener
1 large orange, juiced

For the yogurt ice

340 g bag frozen raspberries
1 tablespoon artificial sweetener
500 g (1 lb 2 oz) 0% fat Greek yogurt

2½ *POINTS* values per serving
9½ *POINTS* values per recipe

163 calories per serving

Takes **10 minutes** to prepare,
15 minutes to cook + **1 hour** freezing

V

✱ recommended (for the yogurt ice only)

1 Make the yogurt ice by blending the frozen raspberries and sweetener and half the yogurt (250 g/9 oz) in a food processor or blender. Fold in the rest of the yogurt until you have a ripple effect, then tip the mixture into a freezer container. Cover and freeze for 1 hour before serving.

2 Meanwhile, preheat the oven to Gas Mark 4/180°C/fan oven 160°C. Arrange the pineapple slices in an ovenproof dish and sprinkle over the crushed cardamom, sweetener and orange juice. Bake for 15 minutes or until golden and caramelized.

3 Serve two slices of pineapple with three scoops of the raspberry ice, per serving.

Tips To tell if a pineapple is ripe, smell it. Only if it smells strongly is it ripe.

The yogurt ice can be kept in the freezer for several weeks and used with other desserts.

Variation Use 8 peeled and sliced clementines instead of the pineapple, for 2 *POINTS* values per serving.

Plum Tarte Tatin

This French upside down tart is a real winner. Serve barely warm for the best flavour, accompanied by the chilled half fat crème fraîche.

Serves 6

75 g (2¾ oz) granulated sugar
4 tablespoons just boiled water
500 g (1 lb 2 oz) plums, halved and stoned
4 x 15 g sheets filo pastry
low fat cooking spray
6 tablespoons half fat crème fraîche, to serve

3 *POINTS* values per serving
18½ *POINTS* values per recipe

150 calories per serving

Takes **40 minutes** to prepare,
20 minutes to cook + cooling

V

✻ not recommended

1 Put the sugar and 3 tablespoons of cold water into a 19–22 cm (7½–8½ inch) heavy based frying pan that will withstand oven temperatures or use a tarte tatin dish. Cook steadily over a medium heat, without stirring, until the sugar caramelises and turns a rich amber colour. Keep a careful eye on the pan, as the sugar continues to cook and can easily burn.

2 Being very careful, pour the hot water into the pan. The mixture will bubble up, but it will soon settle. If the mixture solidifies, cook over a low heat for 1–2 minutes to make sure that the caramel has melted.

3 Add the plums to the pan, packing them in so they are level with the rim of the pan. Cook over a low heat for 8–10 minutes, so that the plums cook in the caramel sauce. Remove the pan from the heat and cool completely. This will take about 30 minutes.

4 Preheat the oven to Gas Mark 5/190°C/fan oven 170°C.

5 Cut the filo pastry sheets in half to form squares. Spray each piece with the cooking spray and stack them into one pile. Place the stack on top of the frying pan to cover the plums. Trim around the edge, allowing an overhang of about 1 cm (½ inch). Tuck this overhang inside the pan.

6 Stand the pan on a baking sheet and transfer it to the middle shelf of the oven. Bake for 15–20 minutes, until the pastry is light golden brown. Cool for 10 minutes and then run a knife around the edge to loosen the pastry. Place a large serving plate over the pan – hold it firmly – and invert the pan to release the tart on to the plate.

7 Slice the tarte into six portions. Serve each slice with 1 tablespoon of half fat crème fraîche.

Apple and Walnut Pie

Nothings beats an apple pie. This version has walnuts added to give an extra twist.

Serves 8

25 g (1 oz) walnut pieces
25 g (1 oz) butter
50 g (1¾ oz) caster sugar
1 egg
finely grated zest and juice of a small lemon
25 g (1 oz) self raising flour
1 teaspoon ground cinnamon
8 crisp eating apples (e.g. Cox), peeled, cored
  and sliced
1 tablespoon sultanas
270 g packet filo pastry sheets
low fat cooking spray
1 teaspoon icing sugar, sifted, for dusting

4 *POINTS* values per serving
32½ *POINTS* values per recipe

231 calories per serving

Takes 25 minutes to prepare,
1 hour to cook

V

 recommended

1 Preheat the oven to Gas Mark 5/190°C/fan oven 170°C. Place the walnuts on a non stick baking tray and bake in the oven for 5–10 minutes until golden and toasted. Whizz the nuts in a food processor until chopped finely.

2 In a small bowl, cream together the butter and 40 g (1½ oz) of the sugar.

3 Whisk in the egg, then the lemon zest, flour and ½ teaspoon of the cinnamon. Finally, mix in the nuts.

4 Put the apples in a large bowl and toss with the lemon juice, sultanas and the remaining sugar and cinnamon.

5 Line a 23 cm (9 inch) metal flan dish with three quarters of the pastry. Use the cooking spray to spray the part of each sheet that will form the base of the pie. Allow the unsprayed edges to overhang.

6 Spread the nut mixture over the base then top the with the apple slices. Gather up the overhanging pastry, scrunching up the sheets like paper. Scrunch up the remaining pastry and use to completely conceal the apple filling.

7 Lightly spray the top of the pie with the cooking spray. Bake for 50–60 minutes. Cover with foil if the pastry starts to brown too much.

8 Serve warm, dusted with the sieved icing sugar.

Raspberry Slice

Create a spectacular raspberry dessert cake – without it having a spectacular effect on your waistline.

Serves 8

low fat cooking spray
5 x 45 g sheets filo pastry
250 g (9 oz) Quark
300 g (10½ oz) low fat soft cheese
1 teaspoon vanilla extract
3 tablespoons artificial sweetener
250 g (9 oz) raspberries, defrosted if frozen
2 teaspoons icing sugar, for dusting

 3 *POINTS* values per serving
22 *POINTS* values per recipe

C **175 calories** per serving

Takes **30 minutes** to prepare,
6 minutes to cook

V

✳ recommended

1 Preheat the oven to Gas Mark 6/200°C/fan oven 180°C. Spray three baking trays with the cooking spray. (If you only have one or two baking trays, you can cook the pastry in batches).

2 Place one sheet of filo pastry on to a work surface and spray with the cooking spray. Pile the rest of the filo pastry sheets on top, spraying in between each sheet with the cooking spray. Using a sharp knife or scissors, cut the pile into three stacks, each measuring approximately 25 x 12.5 cm (10 x 5 inches). Place each stack of pastry sheets on to a baking tray.

3 Bake the filo pastry stacks for 5–6 minutes, or until golden brown. Remove from the oven and leave until completely cold.

4 Beat the Quark, soft cheese, vanilla extract and sweetener together. Crush half the raspberries lightly with a fork, then fold them gently through the mixture – there is no need to mix them in thoroughly.

5 Put one stack of filo pastry sheets on to a serving platter. Spread half the raspberry mixture over the surface and scatter half the remaining raspberries on top. Position one more stack of filo pastry on top, then carefully spoon the rest of the raspberry mixture over, spreading it out to the edges. Add the remaining raspberries. Position the rest of the filo pastry sheets on top. Serve, sprinkled with the icing sugar.

Compote of Dried Fruit

This French recipe makes a tasty and nutritious dessert. It's also delicious served with 1 tablespoon of low fat natural yogurt per person, for an extra ½ *POINTS* value per serving.

Serves 4

115 g (4 oz) dried apricots
250 g can prunes in juice, drained
115 g (4 oz) dried peaches or pears, halved
115 g (4 oz) dried figs, halved
60 g (2 oz) sultanas
100 g (3½ oz) sugar
2 tablespoons orange flower water or rose water
  (optional)

1 Wash all the fruit and then put it in a lidded saucepan with 1 litre (1¾ pints) of water and the sugar. Bring to the boil, then cover and simmer for 15 minutes.

2 Leave to cool for at least 30 minutes, then add the orange flower water or rose water, if using. Transfer to a bowl and refrigerate until needed.

 5½ *POINTS* values per serving
21½ *POINTS* values per recipe

C **355 calories** per serving

Takes **5 minutes** to prepare,
15 minutes to cook + **30 minutes** cooling

V

 not recommended

Serving suggestion Serve sprinkled with 2 tablespoons chopped pistachio nuts, for an extra ½ *POINTS* value per serving.

Fruit Bakes

Polenta might seem like an unusual topping, but give these little autumnal bakes a try, they are really tasty.

Serves 2

2 tablespoons artificial sweetener
½ vanilla pod, seeds scraped out
2 pears, cored and sliced
75 g (2¾ oz) fresh blackberries

200 ml (7 fl oz) skimmed milk
50 g (1¾ oz) dried polenta
low fat cooking spray
200 g pot low fat natural yogurt,
  to serve

1 Preheat the oven to Gas Mark 5/190°C/fan oven 170°C. For the vanilla syrup, mix 2 tablespoons of water with 1 tablespoon of sweetener and the vanilla seeds. Set aside.

2 Divide the pears and blackberries between two 250 ml (9 fl oz) ovenproof dishes and pour over the vanilla syrup.

3 Put the milk in a saucepan and bring to the boil. Quickly stir in the polenta and remaining artificial sweetener and stir until thickened. Pour on top of the fruits, spray with the cooking spray and bake in the oven for 30 minutes until golden. Serve with the yogurt.

3½ *POINTS* values per serving
7 *POINTS* values per recipe

C **265 calories** per serving

Takes **15 minutes** to prepare,
30 minutes to bake

V

* not recommended

Strawberry Salad

This may sound like an odd combination but it is very refreshing and makes a sophisticated party dessert.

Serves 4

400 g (14 oz) strawberries, hulled and sliced thinly
¼ teaspoon balsamic vinegar
2 tablespoons caster sugar
2 teaspoons finely chopped fresh mint
sprigs of mint, to decorate

1 POINTS value per serving
3½ POINTS values per recipe

55 calories per serving

Takes **5 minutes** + **1 hour** chilling

V

∗ not recommended

1 Put the strawberries in a bowl and sprinkle with the other ingredients, except the mint sprigs.

2 Chill for 1 hour.

3 Decorate with the sprigs of mint and serve.

Boozy Sticky Toffee Bananas

This recipe is an excellent way of using up bananas when they've gone past their best.

Serves 2

15 g (½ oz) low fat spread
a pinch of ground cinnamon
1 tablespoon golden syrup
2 tablespoons dark rum
2 bananas

3 *POINTS* values per serving
6 *POINTS* values per recipe

C **207 calories** per serving

Takes **20 minutes**

V

✳ not recommended

1 Melt the low fat spread in a small, non stick frying pan and add the cinnamon, golden syrup and rum. Cook until the mixture bubbles.

2 Slice the bananas in half lengthways and then cut across each half. Add the banana pieces to the pan and cook for 5–8 minutes, spooning the pan juices over the bananas, until they begin to soften.

3 Serve the bananas with the pan juices spooned over them.

Tip This is delicious served with 1 tablespoon of half fat crème fraîche per person, for an extra 1½ *POINTS* values per serving.

Greek Fruit Brûlée

This is a delicious twist on a traditional crème brûlée.

Serves 4

2 peaches, stoned and cut into chunks
100 g (3½ oz) seedless grapes, halved
50 g (1¾ oz) mango, cut into chunks
2 kiwi fruit, peeled and each cut into 8 pieces
300 g (10½ oz) 0% fat Greek yogurt
75 g (2¾ oz) light brown or demerara sugar

2½ **POINTS** values per serving
9½ **POINTS** values per recipe

168 **calories** per serving

Takes **15 minutes** + at least **1 hour** chilling

V

* not recommended

1 Arrange the fruit in the bottom of one large flameproof dish (see Tip). Spoon over the Greek yogurt and smooth the top to cover as much of the fruit as possible. Chill in the fridge for at least an hour.

2 Preheat the grill to its maximum heat. Sprinkle the sugar over the yogurt and place the dish under the grill for 2–4 minutes or until the sugar has caramelised. It's best to do this as quickly as possible, so put your dish as close to the grill as you can. Alternatively, if you have a cook's blow torch, you can use that to caramelise the sugar. Serve immediately.

Tip A Pyrex or soufflé dish is ideal for this recipe. The deeper and narrower the dish, the thicker the layers will be (which is particularly good for the caramel layer). You could also use four smaller flameproof dishes or ramekins. Caster sugar will caramelise well, but does not have the extra depth of flavour or colour that the brown sugars have.

Hot Spiced Fruit Salad

Fruit salads are just as good served hot. Dried fruits soaked in rum and spice mix well with autumnal fruits such as apples, pears and plums. Serve this salad warm for the best flavour.

Serves 4

227 g can apricots in natural juice

2 tablespoons rum

1 teaspoon mixed spice or ½ teaspoon ground cinnamon

75 g (2¾ oz) dried cranberries

50 g (1¾ oz) raisins

1 large, unpeeled dessert apple (e.g Cox or Braeburn), cored and sliced

1 large, unpeeled dessert pear, cored and sliced

2 ripe red plums, stoned and sliced

2½ **POINTS** values per serving
10 **POINTS** values per recipe

160 **calories** per serving

Takes **15 minutes**

V

* recommended

1 Put the apricots and their juice in a medium size saucepan with the rum and mixed spice or cinnamon and heat for 2 minutes. Mix in the dried fruits.

2 Mix the fresh fruits into the hot fruit mixture and spoon the fruit salad into four serving dishes.

Variation You can omit the rum if you like and add a teaspoon of vanilla essence instead. The **POINTS** values will be 2 per serving.

Light as a Feather

Meringues, soufflés, fools and whips – all light and delicious and sure to impress.
Try Floating Meringues, Lemon Berry Soufflé, Blueberry Fools or Raspberry and
Passion Fruit Meringues.

Whip up a light dessert for a
melt-in-the-mouth experience

Baked Apple and Blackberry Meringues

Try this fabulous pudding in autumn when blackberries are up for grabs in the hedgerows and apples are plentiful, local and cheap.

Serves 4

100 g (3½ oz) fresh blackberries
2 tablespoons artificial sweetener
4 cooking apples

For the meringue
2 egg whites
4 tablespoons artificial sweetener

1 *POINTS* value per serving
3½ *POINTS* values per recipe

C **95 calories** per serving

Takes **10 minutes** to prepare,
40 minutes to cook

V

✱ recommended (blackberry and apple mixture only)

1 Preheat the oven to Gas Mark 4/180°C/fan oven 160°C. In a small bowl, mix the blackberries with the sweetener. Core the apples, slice off the bottom so that the apples sit firmly and score the skin around the tops with a sharp knife.

2 Place the apples on a baking tray and spoon the blackberry mixture into the central cavities. Bake for 30 minutes.

3 Meanwhile, make the meringue. In a clean, grease-free bowl, whisk the egg whites until they form stiff peaks. Then add the sweetener, half at a time, whisking between additions.

4 Remove the apples from the oven and turn the heat up to Gas Mark 6/200°C/fan oven 180°C. When cool enough to handle, strip off the top half of the apple skin and spoon some meringue on the top of each one.

5 Return to the oven for a further 5–10 minutes or until the meringue is crisp and golden.

Lemon Berry Soufflé

A great make-ahead recipe that looks like a soufflé but is actually a variation on a chilled mousse. So this is one soufflé you can be confident will never sink.

Serves 6

finely grated zest and juice of 2 lemons
6 eggs, separated
300 g (10½ oz) frozen forest fruits
2 sachets of gelatine
5 tablespoons artificial sweetener
300 g (10½ oz) low fat berry or cherry fruit
  flavoured yogurt
6 mint leaves, to decorate (optional)

2½ *POINTS* values per serving
14½ *POINTS* values per recipe

155 calories per serving

Takes **30 minutes** + chilling

✱ not recommended

1 Place the lemon zest and juice in a large bowl with the egg yolks. Stand the bowl over a saucepan of simmering water and whisk until it begins to thicken to a custard. This will take 5–10 minutes. Put to one side to cool slightly.

2 Put the frozen fruits in a lidded saucepan without any water. Cover, bring them up to a simmer, then remove the lid, mash the fruits with a fork and increase the heat. Boil away most of the excess liquid for 3–5 minutes or so until you're left with a thick slush.

3 Meanwhile, put 4 tablespoons of hot water in a small, wide dish and sprinkle the gelatine over it. Leave for 5 minutes (see Tip).

4 Whisk the gelatine, the fruit pulp, the sweetener and the yogurt into the custard mixture and put into a fridge to chill for 15–30 minutes or until the custard is visibly starting to set.

5 Prepare six 8 cm (3¼ inch) ramekin dishes by cutting six strips of baking parchment. Fix these around the ramekins in a collar that sits above the dish by at least 2½ cm (1 inch).

6 Wash and dry the whisks thoroughly and, in a clean, grease-free bowl, whisk the egg whites until they form stiff peaks. Using a metal spoon, carefully fold them into the custard. Divide this mixture between the six ramekin dishes so that the mixture comes a little higher than the edge of the ramekin dish and is held in by the collar. Place in a fridge to chill for at least 2 hours. Just before serving, carefully remove the collar and decorate with the mint, if using.

Tip When your gelatine is ready to use it should be a light amber colour and all the grains should have dissolved. If it still looks lumpy, even after stirring, pop it in the microwave for just a few seconds and stir again. Alternatively, put the dish in a bowl of very hot water and stir. Never let the mixture boil.

Summer Fruit Whip

In the summertime when soft fruits are plentiful, this dessert can be made in batches and frozen in individual portions; it's actually delicious eaten frozen too.

Serves 4

350 g bag packet frozen mixed summer fruits or mixed fresh soft fruits

25 g (1 oz) caster sugar

350 g (12 oz) low fat natural fromage frais

2 tablespoons reduced sugar strawberry or raspberry jam

2½ POINTS values per serving
10 POINTS values per recipe

105 calories per serving

Takes **30 minutes**

V

✳ recommended

1 Allow the fruit to defrost, if frozen, for about half an hour; they don't need to be completely defrosted.

2 Place the fruit in a food processor with the sugar, fromage frais and jam. Blend for about 30 seconds and then transfer to serving dishes and serve at once.

Black Forest Meringue Pudding

This is a sweet tooth's dream of a pudding and so quick to make. It combines juice-soaked bread and tart berries crowned with a cloud of meringue. Serve hot with 1 tablespoon half fat crème fraîche per person, for an extra 1½ **POINTS** values per serving.

Serves 4

500 g bag frozen Black Forest fruits, defrosted
8 tablespoons artificial sweetener
2 slices wholemeal bread
2 large egg whites

1 **POINTS** value per serving
4½ **POINTS** values per recipe

C **90 calories** per serving

Takes **15 minutes** to prepare,
10 minutes to cook

V

* not recommended

1 Preheat the oven to Gas Mark 5/190°C/fan oven 170°C. Place the fruit and 4 tablespoons of sweetener in a medium sized, lidded saucepan. Cover the pan and heat the fruit through.

2 Meanwhile, line the base of 1.2 litre (2 pint) baking dish with the sliced bread. Pour over the fruit and the juice and spread them about evenly.

3 In a clean, grease-free bowl, whisk the egg whites until they form stiff peaks, then whisk in the remaining sweetener so that you have a thick and glossy meringue mixture. Pile on top of the fruit and spread out to cover.

4 Bake in the oven for 10 minutes, or until the meringue is crisp and a pale brown colour and the fruit is bubbling up at the edges.

Light Apple Fluff

A light and fluffy fruity dessert that's easy to prepare ahead, and the perfect recipe for using up those windfall apples.

Serves 4

700 g (1 lb 9 oz) cooking apples, peeled, cored and chopped
½ teaspoon ground cinnamon
4 tablespoons artificial sweetener
100 g (3½ oz) low fat natural yogurt
1 egg white
1 dessert apple, cored and sliced, to decorate

 1 *POINTS* value per serving
4 *POINTS* values per recipe

C **98 calories** per serving

🕐 Takes **20 minutes** + chilling

V

✳ not recommended

1 Place the cooking apples in a lidded saucepan with the cinnamon and 2 tablespoons of water. Cover the pan and cook gently for 10 minutes, stirring occasionally, until the apples have softened to a purée. Transfer to a mixing bowl, stir in the sweetener and leave to cool.

2 Stir the yogurt into the cooled apple purée.

3 In a clean, grease-free bowl, whisk the egg white until it forms soft peaks and then fold it into the apple mixture using a metal spoon. Divide between four dessert dishes, cover with cling film and chill for 1 hour.

4 Top with the sliced apple before serving.

Tip When beating egg whites, always start your mixer on a low speed then gradually increase the speed once they are frothy. This creates many small bubbles rather than fewer large ones, giving a more stable structure, which is especially important when making a meringue mixture.

Baked Strawberry Alaskas

These mini baked alaskas will go down a treat with the family and are smart enough for a dinner party too.

Serves 4

4 x 25 g (1¾ oz) slices of Swiss jam roll
1 ripe peach or nectarine, skinned and stoned
2 tablespoons sherry
250 g (9 oz) strawberries, all but 4 hulled and sliced thinly
1 egg white
50 g (1¾ oz) caster sugar
4 x 60 g (2 oz) scoops low fat vanilla ice cream
mint leaves, to garnish (optional)

4 POINTS values per serving
15½ POINTS values per recipe

199 calories per serving

Takes **20 minutes**

V

✱ not recommended

1 Preheat the grill to medium high. Place the Swiss roll slices in the bases of four small ramekin dishes.

2 Mash or liquidise the peach or nectarine with the sherry. Spoon the purée over the sponge bases and top with the sliced strawberries.

3 For the meringue, in a clean, grease-free bowl, whisk the egg white until it forms stiff peaks, then whisk in the sugar, a little at a time, until the meringue becomes glossy.

4 For each dish, spoon a scoop of the ice cream on top of the fruits, then swirl over a quarter of the meringue. Make sure that the meringue forms a seal around the edge of each ramekin dish.

5 Flash under the grill just until the meringue is tinged golden brown. Serve immediately, topped with a whole strawberry and a few mint leaves, if using.

Variation Replace the strawberries with fresh raspberries. The **POINTS** values will remain the same.

Hot Banana Soufflés

Bananas are one of the nation's favourite fruit. Try this recipe for the proof of the pudding – a hot and fluffy soufflé that is very easy to make and looks most impressive.

Serves 4

15 g (½ oz) butter, softened
50 g (1¾ oz) caster sugar
3 ripe bananas
juice of ½ a lemon
4 egg whites

© **2½ POINTS** values per serving
10½ POINTS values per recipe

C **175 calories** per serving

⊙ Takes **15 minutes** to prepare,
10 minutes to cook

V

✱ not recommended

1 Preheat the oven to Gas Mark 4/180°C/fan oven 160°C. Wipe the inside of four individual ramekin dishes (approximately 9 cm/3½ inch diameter) with the softened butter, then sprinkle with 1 tablespoon of sugar, swirling each ramekin until well coated.

2 Using a blender or hand held blender, whizz the bananas with half the lemon juice until you have a smooth purée. Set aside.

3 In a clean, grease-free bowl, whisk the egg whites and a few drops of the remaining lemon juice to form soft peaks. Gradually add the remaining sugar and lemon juice until you have firm white peaks.

4 Whisk one quarter of the egg whites into the banana purée (this helps to loosen the purée), then fold in the remainder carefully.

5 Fill each ramekin with the banana mixture, smoothing over the top. Run your thumb around the inner edge of each ramekin to push the mixture away from the sides.

6 Place on a baking sheet and cook for 8–10 minutes until well risen. Serve immediately.

Tip Ripe bananas are sweeter because more of their starch has been converted to sugar – without changing the **POINTS** values.

Strawberry Cloud

This very easy light-as-air dessert is perfect if you grow your own strawberries, though it makes a few go a long way.

Serves 6

225 g (8 oz) strawberries, hulled
1 egg white
75 g (2¾ oz) icing sugar
1 tablespoon lemon juice
6 After Eight mints, cut in half to form triangles

1½ *POINTS* values per serving
9 *POINTS* values per recipe

95 calories per serving

Takes **25 minutes** + chilling

V

✱ not recommended

1 Wash the strawberries and pat dry thoroughly with kitchen paper. Put them into a bowl and mash with a fork or potato masher.

2 In a clean, grease-free bowl, whisk the egg white until it forms stiff peaks, then gradually whisk in the icing sugar.

3 Gradually whisk in the strawberries, then whisk on high speed for 4–5 minutes until the mixture is light, foamy and thick. Whisk in the lemon juice, then spoon into six individual dishes.

4 Cover and chill in the refrigerator until ready to serve. Decorate each one with an After Eight mint.

Tip You can make this dessert in advance, allowing it to chill in the refrigerator overnight.

Variations Make up a strawberry or lemon-flavoured sugar-free jelly and set in the bottom of six tall serving glasses, then top with Strawberry Cloud, for no extra *POINTS* values.

Instead of the mints, sprinkle each dessert with a tiny amount of cocoa powder. This will reduce the *POINTS* values to 1 per serving.

Raspberry and Passion Fruit Meringues

Exotic flavoured passion fruit seeds and raspberries set off the sweetness of these meringues. Serve the meringues on the day of baking, to retain their crisp texture.

Serves 4

4 egg whites
6 level tablespoons artificial sweetener
2 x 150 g cartons 0% fat Greek yogurt
150 g (5½ oz) raspberries
2 passion fruit, halved

 1 POINTS value per serving
3 POINTS values per recipe

C **85 calories** per serving

🕐 Takes **5 minutes** to prepare,
1 hour to cook

V

✱ not recommended

1 Preheat the oven to Gas Mark ½/120°C/fan oven 100°C. Line a baking tray with baking parchment.

2 In a clean, grease-free bowl, whisk the egg whites until they form stiff peaks, then whisk in the sweetener until you get a thick and glossy mixture.

3 Spoon four mounds on to the prepared tray, then use a dampened spoon to shape them into rounds and hollow out the centre to make meringue nests.

4 Bake in the oven for 1 hour, then leave to cool.

5 Spoon the yogurt into the centre of each meringue, top with raspberries and the seeds of half a passion fruit each. Serve immediately.

Queen of Puddings

This light version of the traditional British recipe is just perfect to finish off a family supper.

Serves 4

250 ml (9 fl oz) skimmed milk
50 g (1¾ oz) oat bran
finely grated zest of a lemon
4 tablespoons artificial sweetener
150 g (5½ oz) fresh blueberries
250 g (9 oz) fresh raspberries
3 eggs, separated

 2 *POINTS* values per serving
9 *POINTS* values per recipe

C 160 calories per serving

Takes **20 minutes** to prepare,
40 minutes to cook + **30 minutes** soaking

V

✳ not recommended

1 Heat the milk in a pan and bring just to the boil. Remove from the heat and add the oat bran, lemon zest and 1 tablespoon of sweetener. Leave to soak for 30 minutes.

2 Meanwhile, put the blueberries and raspberries into another small pan and gently cook, stirring for 5 minutes until half the fruits have burst, releasing their juices. Set aside.

3 Preheat the oven to Gas Mark 4/180°C/fan oven 160°C. Beat the egg yolks into the soaked oat bran and pour into a 1 litre (1¾ pint) ovenproof dish. Bake for 30 minutes until just set. Then spread the cooked fruits over the oat mixture.

4 In a clean, grease-free bowl, whisk the egg whites until foamy. Gradually whisk in the remaining sweetener until stiff peaks are formed. Spoon over the top of the pudding, creating peaks with the back of a spoon (don't worry about spreading the meringue up against the edges – it's quite pretty to see some of the fruits) and bake in the oven for 10 minutes until golden.

Floating Meringues

Sweet, soft meringues floating on a sea of vanilla custard.

Serves 4

1 vanilla pod
400 ml (14 fl oz) skimmed milk
6 eggs, separated
6 tablespoons artificial sweetener
fine strips of zest from a lemon, to decorate

2½ **POINTS** values per serving
9 **POINTS** values per recipe

C **186 calories** per serving

Takes **30 minutes** to prepare + infusing

V

✳ not recommended

1 Use a sharp knife to split the vanilla pod in half lengthways. Scrape out the seeds and retain both pod and seeds.

2 Heat the milk to nearly boiling in a lidded saucepan, stirring continuously. Remove from the heat, add the vanilla seeds and pod, cover and leave to infuse for at least 10 minutes before removing the pod.

3 Whisk the eggs yolks together in a large bowl. Reheat the milk gently until it just starts to steam. Pour the hot milk in a steady stream over the egg yolks while beating. Return the milk and egg mixture to the saucepan. Stir and heat very gently until the custard thickens enough to coat the back of a spoon. This will take about 5 minutes – do not boil the custard or it will separate. Remove from the heat and pour into a cold bowl. Stir in 2 tablespoons of sweetener and allow the custard to cool. Stir occasionally to avoid a skin forming.

4 Bring a large saucepan of water to a gentle simmer. In a clean, grease-free bowl, whisk the egg whites until they form stiff peaks. Whisk in the remaining sweetener.

5 Using a metal tablespoon, lift a spoonful of meringue mixture from the bowl and lower it as neatly as you can into the simmering water. Poach it uncovered for 45 seconds, turn it gently with the spoon and poach for a further 45 seconds on the other side. (If you cook them for any longer they get too moist and will flatten and shrink as they cool.) Remove the meringue to a plate covered with kitchen paper to soak up excess moisture. Repeat with the remaining mixture, poaching several at a time if you like. You only need eight 'meringues', so you can select the eight best shaped ones.

6 Once all the meringue is cooked, share the custard between four bowls and place the meringues on top. Decorate with the thin strips of lemon zest and your 'floating meringues' are ready to serve at room temperature when it suits you.

Raspberry Fluff

This is a variation of a traditional Scottish dessert. Usually made with cream and honey, this version is low in **POINTS** values and just as delicious.

Serves 4

100 g (3½ oz) oatmeal
175 g (6 oz) fresh raspberries
2–3 teaspoons artificial sweetener
175 g (6 oz) very low fat natural fromage frais
1 tablespoon whisky
mint sprigs, to decorate

---

2 POINTS values per serving
8 POINTS values per recipe

C   **140 calories** per serving

Takes **20 minutes**

V

✳   not recommended

1   Heat the grill to medium high and toast the oatmeal under the grill for 2–3 minutes until golden. Do not let it burn or it will taste bitter. Leave to cool.

2   In a large bowl, mix the raspberries, reserving a few for decoration, with a teaspoon of sweetener. Add the fromage frais, whisky and the remaining sweetener to taste.

3   Layer the raspberry mixture with the oatmeal in four serving glasses. Decorate with the reserved raspberries and mint sprigs, and serve at once.

White Chocolate and Redcurrant Pavlovas

Individual pavlova cases filled with a sweet white chocolate cream and crowned with tart little redcurrants to provide the perfect balance.

Serves 8

4 egg whites
a pinch of cream of tartar
100 g (3½ oz) caster sugar

For the filling
75 g (2¾ oz) white chocolate, broken into pieces
2 tablespoons condensed skimmed milk
200 g (7 oz) low fat soft cheese
100 g (3½ oz) sprigs of fresh redcurrants

 2½ POINTS values per serving
21 POINTS values per recipe

C **150 calories** per serving

Takes **25 minutes** to prepare,
1 hour to cook + cooling

V

✱ not recommended

1 Preheat the oven to Gas Mark ½/120°C/fan oven 100°C. In a clean, grease-free bowl, whisk the egg whites with the cream of tartar until they form soft peaks. Whisk in half the sugar, then the other half and whisk again until stiff and glossy.

2 Line two baking sheets with baking parchment and pencil on eight 15 cm (3 inch) circles. Either pipe or spoon the meringue to cover the circles, building up the edges slightly to make shallow nests. Bake for 1 hour.

3 Leave to cool on the paper and then peel off the paper carefully.

4 Meanwhile, place the chocolate pieces into a heatproof bowl and set over a pan of simmering water, making sure the water does not touch the bottom of the bowl. Melt the chocolate, stirring occasionally.

5 To make the filling, beat together the melted chocolate, milk and soft cheese until smooth then spoon into the pavlovas. Top with the redcurrants and serve.

Tip For a quick dessert, use shop bought meringue nests. The **POINTS** values will remain the same.

Pineapple Meringues with Strawberry Sauce

This easy and impressive dessert only takes minutes to put together and it tastes fantastic.

Serves 4

1 small fresh pineapple
350 g (12 oz) strawberries, hulled and sliced
2 kiwi fruit, peeled and sliced
2 egg whites
25 g (1 oz) caster sugar

1½ *POINTS* values per serving
5½ *POINTS* values per recipe

C **100 calories** per serving

Takes **15 minutes**

V

✳ not recommended

1 Preheat the oven to Gas Mark 5/190°C/fan oven 170°C.

2 Cut the pineapple into four thick slices and remove the core, using a sharp knife or a small biscuit cutter to make it easier. Place the slices on a non stick baking sheet.

3 Reserve half the strawberries and mix the remainder with the kiwi fruit. Pile on top of the pineapple slices.

4 In a clean, grease-free bowl, whisk the egg whites until they form stiff peaks and then add the sugar and whisk again until stiff and glossy. Pile on top of the strawberries and kiwi.

5 Transfer to the oven at once and bake for about 4–5 minutes, until golden brown. Meanwhile, purée the reserved strawberries in a blender or using a hand held blender.

6 Serve the meringues, drizzled with the strawberry sauce.

Variation Substitute any fresh fruit for the strawberries and kiwi fruit. For a tropical flavour, you could try a combination of mango and papaya, for a *POINTS* value of 2 per serving.

Blueberry Fools

Blueberries are deliciously sweet. Blitz them with yogurt and fromage frais for a quick and nutritious fruit fool.

Serves 2

150 g (5½ oz) blueberries
50 g (1¾ oz) 0% fat Greek yogurt
75 g (2¾ oz) fat free natural fromage frais
2 teaspoons artificial sweetener

1 POINTS value per serving
2 POINTS values per recipe

C **61 calories** per serving

Takes **5 minutes**
+ **1 hour 10 minutes** chilling

V

* not recommended

1 Reserving 8–10 blueberries for decoration, place the remainder in the microwave and cook on High for 1 minute, then cool to room temperature for 1 hour.

2 Place the cooled blueberries in a blender, or use a hand held blender, and whizz until roughly blended.

3 Mix together the yogurt, fromage frais and sweetener. Spoon the blueberries into a bowl and stir through the yogurt mixture, creating a swirly effect. Chill for 10 minutes before serving in glass bowls decorated with the reserved blueberries.

Strawberry Soufflé Omelette

When you want something filling but fancy, and sweet rather than savoury, this fits the bill.

Serves 1

2 eggs, separated
2 tablespoons skimmed milk
1 teaspoon caster sugar
100 g (3½ oz) fresh strawberries, hulled and sliced
1 tablespoon reduced sugar strawberry jam
low fat cooking spray

4 POINTS values per serving
4 POINTS values per recipe

270 calories per serving

Takes **25 minutes**

V

✱ not recommended

1 In a medium sized bowl, beat the egg yolks with the milk and caster sugar.

2 In a clean, grease-free bowl, whisk the egg whites until they form stiff peaks. Fold them into the egg yolk mixture.

3 Mix the sliced strawberries with the strawberry jam and set aside.

4 Spray a 19 cm (7½ inch) lidded, non stick frying pan with the cooking spray and add the egg mixture. Cover and cook over a medium to low heat for 5 minutes, until the egg begins to set.

5 Scatter the strawberry mixture over the omelette and, using a wooden spatula, fold one side of the omelette over the other. Transfer it to a warmed plate and eat at once.

Peach Melba Soufflé Omelette

A super fast variation on the Strawberry Soufflé Omelette (opposite) creating a delicious dessert for two.

Serves 2

150 g (5½ oz) raspberries

2 teaspoons artificial sweetener, plus extra for dusting

2 peaches, stoned and sliced

3 eggs, separated

low fat cooking spray

 **2½ POINTS** values per serving
5½ POINTS values per recipe

C **196 calories** per serving

Takes **10 minutes**

V

✳ not recommended

1 Reserve 6 raspberries and mash the rest with a fork. Push the pulp through a sieve to create a purée. Add 1 teaspoon of sweetener.

2 Preheat the grill to high. While the grill is heating, put the peach slices in a flameproof dish and place under the grill to warm through.

3 Meanwhile, in a clean, grease-free bowl, whisk the egg whites until they form stiff peaks. Briefly whisk the yolks in another bowl with the remaining teaspoon of sweetener. Carefully fold the egg whites into the egg yolks with a metal spoon.

4 Heat a non stick frying pan to a medium high temperature and spray with the cooking spray. Pour in the egg mixture and cook for 3 minutes. Then loosen the edges of the omelette with a plastic palette knife or fish slice, checking to see if it is turning just golden brown underneath. Leave it for a further minute if necessary. Remove the peaches from the grill and put the omelette in its pan under the grill. Cook for 1–2 minutes or until the top is golden.

5 Spoon the warm peaches and some of the raspberry purée over half the omelette. Fold over the other half of the omelette and cut in two. Slide on to two plates, drizzle with the remaining raspberry purée and decorate with the reserved raspberries. Dust with sweetener and serve immediately.

Vanilla Mousses with Plums

These vanilla flavoured mousses are like panna cotta, but with far fewer *POINTS* values.

Serves 4

350 ml (12 fl oz) skimmed milk
12 g sachet powdered gelatine
1 vanilla pod
2 tablespoons artificial sweetener
300 g (10½ oz) low fat natural yogurt

For the plums

6 plums, halved and stoned
juice of a large orange
1 teaspoon artificial sweetener

1½ *POINTS* values per serving
7 POINTS values per recipe

137 calories per serving

Takes **15 minutes** to prepare,
25 minutes to cook + **3 hours** chilling

✳ not recommended

1 Measure 4 tablespoons of milk into a small bowl, sprinkle on the gelatine and leave to swell for 5 minutes.

2 Cut the vanilla pod in half and scrape the seeds into the remaining milk in a saucepan. Add the pod. Gently bring the milk to a simmer.

3 Add the soaked gelatine and stir until dissolved. Remove from the heat and stir in the sweetener.

4 Pour into a large mixing bowl and leave to cool for 5 minutes. Remove the vanilla pod at this point.

5 Mix the yogurt into the cooled milk. Pour the mixture into four mini pudding basins or ramekins. Cover and refrigerate for 2–3 hours until set.

6 For the plums, preheat the oven to Gas Mark 5/190°C/fan oven 170°C. Place the plums in an ovenproof dish, cut side up, pour in the orange juice and sprinkle with sweetener.

7 Roast in the oven for 20–25 minutes, depending on ripeness, until the plums are tender and slightly caramelised. Baste with the juices a couple of times during cooking. Serve the plums warm or cooled, with the turned out mousses.

Tip You can use 1 teaspoon of vanilla extract in step 4 in place of the vanilla pod if you like. The *POINTS* values will remain the same.

Berry Puffs

Little meringue shells encasing a sharp berry purée look great and taste divine.

Serves 4 (makes 10–12 puffs)

low fat cooking spray
100 g (3½ oz) fresh strawberries, hulled
2 egg whites
6 tablespoons artificial sweetener

0 *POINTS* values per serving
½ *POINTS* value per recipe

C   30 calories per serving

Takes **20 minutes** to prepare,
1½ hours to cook

V

✳   not recommended

1 Preheat the oven to Gas Mark ½/120°C/fan oven 100°C. Spray a baking tray with the cooking spray and line it with baking parchment.

2 Place the strawberries in a blender, or use a hand held blender, and whizz them to a purée. Strain them through a sieve to remove the seeds.

3 In a clean, grease-free bowl, whisk the egg whites until they are very dry, white and fluffy. Add the sweetener and whisk again until thoroughly mixed.

4 Place dessertspoons of the meringue mixture well apart on the baking tray and make a slight hollow in the centre of each one with the back of a wet teaspoon. Place a teaspoon of the strawberry purée in each hollow and then top with a blob more of meringue.

5 Bake the meringues for 1½ hours until very slightly golden and crisp on the outside. Serve them with any remaining strawberry purée.

Cool Treats

Far better than shop-bought ice cream, these desserts are perfect for sunny days or special occasions. From a stunning Sicilian Cassata to a grownup Jamaican Rum Pudding, Strawberry Tiramisu or Mango and Lime Parfaits, there is something here for everyone.

Make a cool dessert ahead of time and bring it out at the end of a meal

Mango Cheesecake Sundae

This quick and easy to prepare dessert is the perfect end to any meal.

Serves 4

300 g (10½ oz) low fat soft cheese
200 g (7 oz) 0% fat Greek yogurt
1 tablespoon artificial sweetener
finely grated zest of a lime, plus 1 tablespoon
  lime juice
2 large ripe mangoes
juice of ½ an orange
4 small strawberries or 4 slices of lime,
  to decorate

4 *POINTS* values per serving
16½ *POINTS* values per recipe

C 195 calories per serving

Takes **25 minutes** + chilling

V

✱ not recommended

1 Place the soft cheese, yogurt, sweetener, lime zest and juice in a mixing bowl and beat them together. Chill for at least 30 minutes.

2 Cut both mangoes in half from top to bottom, around the flat stone in their centres. Do the same on the other side of the stone so that that you have two flat slices with the stones in the middle and four mango 'cheeks'. Peel or cut the skin from around the stone slices and chop the fruit away from it. Keep this fruit to one side.

3 Place one of the mango 'cheeks' skin side down. Carefully use a sharp knife to cut through the fruit – but not the skin – centrally from top to bottom. Now cut across the flesh 10 or 12 times to create thin slices. Turn the cheek inside out and the slices will pop up so you can easily skim the knife along the skin to release the slices on to a plate. Repeat with the remaining three 'cheeks'.

4 Take about a quarter of the mango slices and add them to the flesh cut from around the stones. Whizz in a blender, or use a hand held blender, with the orange juice until smooth.

5 When the cheese mixture is well chilled, take four large sundae or Martini style cocktail glasses and put a few slices of mango in the bottom of each glass. Pour over a little of the mango purée, then spoon in a layer of soft cheese mixture. Repeat for two more layers and then top the sundaes with any remaining purée and a strawberry or slice of lime. Chill until ready to serve.

Variation Make Forest Fruit Cheesecake Sundaes by taking 150 g (5½ oz) each of small strawberries, blueberries, blackberries and raspberries. Gently simmer all the fruit, except the raspberries, with 1 tablespoon water for 5 minutes or until the fruit starts to soften. Stir in the raspberries and leave to cool. Once cool, drain off all the excess juice and stir in 2 teaspoons of sweetener. Use this instead of the mangoes and substitute lemon juice and zest instead of the lime in the cream cheese mixture. The ***POINTS*** values will be 3 per serving.

Black Forest Trifle

Everyone loves a Black Forest trifle, and this one has the extra advantage of being low in *POINTS* values too.

Serves 4

500 g bag frozen Black Forest fruits

1 tablespoon caster sugar

1 mulled wine spice bag

2 teaspoons cornflour

20 Weight Watchers Chocolate Brownie Bites, each cut in half

125 ml (4 fl oz) half fat crème fraîche

30 g (1¼ oz) chilled dark chocolate, to decorate

 6 *POINTS* values per serving
23 *POINTS* values per recipe

C 411 calories per serving

Takes **20 minutes** + **10 minutes** cooling

V

✱ not recommended

1 Put half the Black Forest fruits into a bowl and set aside. Put the remaining fruits into a small saucepan with 100 ml (3½ fl oz) of water, the sugar and mulled wine spice bag. Bring to the boil and rapidly boil for 5 minutes. Pass through a sieve into a jug, pressing the fruit with the back of a spoon to squeeze out all the juice. (You should have about 200 ml/7 fl oz juice).

2 Return the fruit juice to a small saucepan. Mix the cornflour to a paste with 1 tablespoon of water and add to the pan. Bring to the boil and simmer for 1 minute, stirring until thickened. Pour this over the reserved frozen fruits in the bowl and leave to cool for 10 minutes.

3 Take four glasses and put four pieces of brownie bites into each glass. Top each glass with a spoonful of the fruit and sauce and then a dollop of half fat crème fraîche. Continue layering, with three pieces of brownie bites in further layers, until everything is used up. Grate the chocolate over each and serve.

Lychee Granita

This fragrant tropical fruit ice is a doddle to make and provides a very refreshing end to a meal. A granita is similar to a sorbet, but has a looser, more granular texture.

Serves 4

425 g can lychees in syrup
3 tablespoons artificial sweetener
juice of a lime
4 mint sprigs, to decorate

1 POINTS value per serving
4 POINTS values per recipe

C **75 calories** per serving

Takes **5 minutes** + approx **4 hours** freezing

V

✱ recommended

1 Tip the lychees and their syrup into a liquidizer, or use a hand held blender, and whizz until smooth. Blend in the sweetener and lime juice.

2 Pour into a shallow, lidded plastic box and freeze for 1–2 hours until the mixture starts to solidify.

3 Remove from the freezer and stir well with a fork to break up the large ice crystals. Return to the freezer for 1 hour, then repeat the process. Freeze until firm.

4 Spoon into individual glasses to serve, decorated with a sprig of mint.

Tip The time the granita will take to freeze depends on your freezer.

Apricot Mousse

This easy to make mousse is perfect following a weekday supper.

Serves 4

150 ml (5 fl oz) boiling water
1 sachet sugar free jelly (flavour of your choice)
410 g can apricots in juice, drained
200 g (7 oz) low fat apricot or natural yogurt

1 POINTS value per serving
5 POINTS values per recipe

80 calories per serving

Takes **10 minutes** + at least **20 minutes** chilling

✱ not recommended

1 Pour the boiling water into a measuring jug. Sprinkle over the jelly powder and stir until dissolved. Leave to cool slightly.

2 Reserving half of the apricots for decoration, blend the rest in a food processor, or use a hand held blender, until smooth. Whisk together the apricot purée and yogurt.

3 When the jelly is only warm, whisk it into the yogurt mixture. Place in the fridge for 20 minutes.

4 Take out and whisk again and divide between four glasses or small bowls.

5 Chill until ready to serve. Slice the remaining apricots in half and use them to decorate the mousses.

Frozen Berry Yogurt

This delicious dessert cleverly uses frozen berries, blitzed in a blender to speed up the preparation time. Serve with 150 g (5½ oz) fresh strawberries or blueberries per person, for an extra ½ **POINTS** value per serving.

Serves 6

350 g (12 oz) raspberries, strawberries and blueberries, or a combination of summer berries, frozen

6 tablespoons artificial sweetener

350 g (12 oz) very low fat natural yogurt

2 teaspoons vanilla extract

---

 1 **POINTS** value per serving
4½ **POINTS** values per recipe

C 58 **calories** per serving

Takes **15 minutes** to prepare,
+ at least **2 hours** chilling

V

✳ recommended

1 In a blender or food processor, whizz the frozen berries until puréed. Add the sweetener, yogurt and vanilla extract and whizz until combined.

2 Tip the mixture into a rigid freezer container and freeze for about 1 hour. Remove and stir with a fork to break up the ice crystals. Repeat every hour until the mixture has frozen. Alternatively, tip the mixture into an ice cream maker and follow the manufacturer's instructions to freeze.

3 Remove the container from the freezer about 30 minutes before serving to allow the mixture to thaw a little. Scoop into small glasses to serve.

Fresh Strawberry Ice Cream

This delicious ice cream is low in *POINTS* values and tastes just as good as any shop bought version.

Serves 8

600 ml (20 fl oz) low fat custard
150 g (5 oz) 0% fat Greek yogurt
200 g (7 oz) strawberries
1 teaspoon caster sugar

1 Mix the custard and yogurt together in a large mixing bowl. Purée the strawberries in a blender or push them through a sieve.

2 Mix the strawberries and sugar with the custard and yogurt mixture. Pour the mixture straight into a freezer proof container and freeze for an hour, and then remove it and beat with a fork to break up the forming ice crystals. Freeze for another half an hour, and then beat again. Continue to do this at half-hour intervals until frozen. Alternatively, pour into an ice cream maker and follow the manufacturer's instructions.

3 Remove the ice cream from the freezer 10 minutes before you want to serve it.

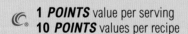

1 *POINTS* value per serving
10 *POINTS* values per recipe

C **85 calories** per serving

Takes **10 minutes** to prepare + freezing

V

✱ recommended

Apple and Pear Sorbet

A simple but unusual sorbet – perfect for a supper party.

Serves 4

4 ripe dessert apples, peeled and cored
4 ripe pears, peeled and cored

juice of a lemon
½ teaspoon ground cinnamon

1 Place the fruit in a medium pan. Pour in enough water just to cover the base of the pan. Simmer for 15–20 minutes or until the fruit is soft. Leave to cool.

2 Place the cooled fruit in a blender or food processor with the lemon juice and cinnamon. Whizz until nearly smooth.

3 Place the sorbet mixture in a freezer proof container and freeze. After 2 hours take out and whisk up with a fork to break up the ice crystals and return to the freezer. Alternatively, pour into an ice cream maker and follow the manufacturer's instructions.

4 Remove from the freezer 10 minutes before you want to serve.

1½ POINTS values per serving
6 POINTS values per recipe

C **111 calories** per serving

Takes **35 minutes** + cooling + **2 hours** freezing

V

✳ recommended

Tip Always allow time for the sorbet to soften before serving.

Mint Kulfi

Kulfi is a rich and creamy Indian ice cream – great for those special occasions.

Serves 8

400 ml (14 fl oz) skimmed milk
397 g can condensed milk
½ teaspoon mint flavouring

---

2 POINTS values per serving
16½ POINTS values per recipe

C **180 calories** per serving

Takes **20 minutes** + freezing

V

* recommended

1 Pour the skimmed milk into a medium, non stick pan and slowly bring to a simmer.

2 Add the condensed milk and bring back to a simmer, stirring constantly. Continue to stir and simmer for 10–12 minutes – the mixture will thicken very slightly.

3 Add the mint flavouring and stir for a couple more minutes.

4 Pour the custard into eight dariole moulds (or similar cone shape moulds that can be frozen) and leave to cool.

5 When cool enough, cover with cling film or foil and place in the freezer for 6–7 hours, or overnight.

6 To serve, remove from the freezer, dip into a bowl of warm water and then tip out on to a plate or shallow dish and serve.

Variations For mango kulfi, purée the flesh of 1 mango and add to the mixture, instead of the mint, before cooling. The **POINTS** values will be 2½ per serving.

Half a teaspoon of menthol liqueur could be used instead of mint flavouring. The **POINTS** values will remain the same.

Grape, Nectarine and Ginger Jellies

These sophisticated jellies make a delicious low **POINTS** value dessert. Enjoy.

Serves 4

100 ml (3½ fl oz) boiling water
1½ tablespoons powdered gelatine
5 cm (2 inches) fresh root ginger, finely grated
800 ml (28 fl oz) white grape juice
3 tablespoons artificial sweetener
150 g (5½ oz) red seedless grapes

To decorate
1 nectarine, thinly sliced
4 sprigs of fresh mint

2 POINTS values per serving
8 POINTS values per recipe

193 calories per serving

Takes **20 minutes** to prepare,
+ **3 hours** chilling

✱ not recommended

1 Pour the boiling water into a jug. Leave it to cool for about 1 minute, then sprinkle the powdered gelatine on top, stirring to disperse it. Leave for about 10 minutes, stirring occasionally, until you have a completely clear liquid.

2 Squeeze the juice from the grated ginger into the gelatine liquid.

3 When the gelatine liquid is cool, add the grape juice, stirring well. Taste a little, adding sweetener if required.

4 Pour the liquid into four glasses and share the grapes between them. Refrigerate until set – about 2–3 hours.

5 When ready to serve, decorate the jellies with the nectarine slices and mint leaves.

Lemon and Lime Cheesecake Pots

These tangy little cheesecake pots feel like a real indulgence.

Serves 4

250 ml (9 fl oz) boiling water
12 g sachet lemon and lime sugar free jelly
juice of ½ a lemon
juice of ½ a lime
150 g (5½ oz) low fat natural yogurt
100 g (3½ oz) low fat soft cheese
100 g (3½ oz) grapes, halved, to decorate

---

1 *POINTS* value per serving
5 *POINTS* values per recipe

C 71 **calories** per serving

Takes **8 minutes** + **15 minutes** cooling
2 hours chilling

✱ not recommended

1 Pour the boiling water into a jug and sprinkle the jelly crystals over, stirring to dissolve. Add the lemon and lime juice, then leave to cool to body temperature, stirring occasionally (this will take about 15 minutes).

2 Mix the yogurt into the soft cheese in a mixing bowl, stirring briskly until smooth. Gradually whisk the cooled jelly into the cheese mixture, until evenly blended. Pour into four ramekins, cover and chill for around 2 hours or until set.

3 Uncover the cheesecake pots and serve topped with the halved grapes.

Instant Raspberry Yogurt Ice Cream

This is the perfect frozen yogurt to refresh you on a hot summer's day or use as a quick accompaniment to fresh fruit.

Serves 4

500 g (1 lb 2 oz) 0% fat Greek yogurt
275 g (9½ oz) frozen raspberries
1 tablespoon icing sugar

1½ POINTS values per serving
6 POINTS values per recipe

C **100 calories** per serving

Takes **20 minutes**

V

✱ recommended

1 Chill four serving glasses in the freezer.

2 Using a blender or hand held blender, whizz all the ingredients together until pink and thick.

3 Pour into the chilled glasses and serve.

Tip Alternatively, pour into a plastic freezer container and freeze until you need it, but remove from the freezer 30 minutes before you want to eat it.

Mango and Lime Parfaits

These parfaits are simple and quick to make and pretty enough to serve to guests.

Serves 4

400 g (14 oz) canned mango slices, drained
200 ml (7 fl oz) mango sorbet
200 ml (7 fl oz) lime or lemon sorbet
100 g (3½ oz) blueberries
2 tablespoons very low fat fromage frais
4 fresh mint sprigs, to decorate

2½ POINTS values per serving
11 POINTS values per recipe

C **203 calories** per serving

Takes **10 minutes**

V

✱ not recommended

1 Put the drained mango into a food processor or blender and whizz to a purée.

2 Place 1 scoop of mango sorbet in each of four dessert or wine glasses. Top each with some of the mango purée and a scoop of lime or lemon sorbet.

3 Add some blueberries and a half tablespoon of fromage frais. Decorate with the remaining blueberries and mint.

Tip You can make your own mango sorbet to use in this recipe. Purée 350 g (12 oz) of mango, add 6 tablespoons of caster sugar, then place the purée in a small pan and heat until boiling. Simmer for a few minutes, with a little water, until the mixture is reduced and thickened. Leave it to cool. In a clean, grease-free bowl, whisk an egg white until it forms stiff peaks, then gently fold it into the cool mango mixture. Pour it into a freezer container and freeze for an hour. Stir to break up any lumps. The **POINTS** values will be 4 per serving. If you wish to have this sorbet on its own, it will be 1½ **POINTS** values per serving (serves 4).

Sicilian Cassata

This frozen ricotta cake is very easy to make and can be made in advance.

Serves 12

8 trifle sponges or sponge fingers

6 tablespoons red fruit juice, e.g. forest fruits or raspberry

250 g (9 oz) ricotta cheese

100 g (3½ oz) icing sugar, sifted

250 g (9 oz) low fat natural yogurt

50 g (1¾ oz) shelled pistachios, chopped

50 g (1¾ oz) ready-to-eat tropical fruit mix, diced finely

100 g (3½ oz) blueberries, washed

150 g (5½ oz) strawberries, hulled, washed and chopped into small pieces

200 g (7 oz) natural colouring glacé cherries, diced finely

a few fresh cherries, to decorate (optional)

 3½ **POINTS** values per serving
44½ **POINTS** values per recipe

C **215 calories** per serving

Takes **10 minutes** + at least **10 hours** freezing

V

✴ recommended

1 Slice the trifle sponges in half lengthways so that they remain the same size but are thinner. Use to line the base of a 23 cm (9 inch) springform cake tin, trimming the sponges to fit the tin so that there are no gaps. Sprinkle the fruit juice over the sponges.

2 In a large bowl, whip the ricotta with the icing sugar until smooth. Then add the yogurt, nuts and all the fruit except the fresh cherries, if using.

3 Spoon on top of the sponges and freeze for at least 10 hours until firm and easy to slice.

4 To serve, carefully remove from the tin on to a plate and garnish with fresh cherries, if using.

Ginger and Orange Cheesecake

The spicy tang of the ginger together with the slight sharpness of the orange makes this a winning combination.

Serves 8

200 ml (7 fl oz) boiling water
1 sachet sugar free orange flavour jelly
300 g (10½ oz) low fat soft cheese
50 g (1¾ oz) caster sugar
150 g (5 oz) 0% fat Greek yogurt
50 g (1¾ oz) stem ginger, drained and chopped finely
2 oranges, peeled and segmented, to decorate

For the base

150 g (5½ oz) reduced fat digestive biscuits, crushed
75 g (2¾ oz) low fat spread, melted
1 teaspoon finely grated orange zest

---

4 POINTS values per serving
33 POINTS values per recipe

C **266 calories** per serving

Takes **15 minutes** + **20 minutes** cooling + **4½ hours** chilling

✱ recommended

1 For the base, mix together the crushed biscuits, low fat spread and orange zest. Press the mixture into the base of a round, loose bottomed, non stick 20 cm (8 inch) cake tin. Chill in the fridge while preparing the filling.

2 Pour the boiling water into a bowl and sprinkle the jelly crystals over, stirring well. Allow to cool for 20 minutes, then whisk in the soft cheese, sugar, yogurt and ginger. Chill the mixture in the refrigerator for 30 minutes.

3 Spoon the cheese mixture over the base. Return to the fridge for at least 4 hours until completely set.

4 Carefully remove the cheesecake from the tin and place it on a serving plate. Decorate the top with the orange segments. Cut into eight wedges to serve.

Variation You can use a 215 g can of mandarin oranges in natural juice, drained, instead of the oranges, to decorate the top if you prefer. The **POINTS** values will remain the same.

Raspberry Sorbet

Make this fabulous sorbet to end a special meal or make it as a low **POINTS** value alternative to Christmas pudding.

Serves 8

225 g (8 oz) frozen raspberries

600 ml (20 fl oz) cranberry and raspberry juice drink

100 g (3½ oz) caster sugar

4 tablespoons sweet sherry

mint leaves, to decorate (optional)

1½ POINTS values per serving
12 POINTS values per recipe

C **110 calories** per serving

Takes **5 minutes** + **2 hours** freezing

V

* recommended

1 Put the frozen raspberries, cranberry and raspberry juice, sugar and sherry into a food processor or liquidiser and blend for about 15 seconds.

2 Turn the mixture out into a rigid freezer proof container and freeze until almost solid, about 1 hour. Turn out and beat well to break up the ice crystals. Return to the freezer and freeze until solid.

3 Before serving, transfer the container to the fridge for about 15 minutes to soften slightly. Scoop into chilled dishes and serve at once, decorated with mint leaves, if using.

Tip If you have an ice-cream maker, use it to prepare the sorbet, following the manufacturer's instructions.

Strawberry Tiramisu

Serve these pretty layered desserts in elegant tall glasses for extra effect.

Serves 2

8 sponge fingers (40 g/1½ oz in total)
4 tablespoons orange juice
150 g (5½ oz) strawberries
125 g (4½ oz) fat free natural fromage frais
1½ tablespoons caster sugar

---

3 POINTS values per serving
5½ POINTS values per recipe

C 187 calories per serving

Takes **20 minutes** to prepare,
+ **20 minutes–1 hour** chilling

V

✱ not recommended

1 Break the sponge fingers into pieces and place half of them in the bottom of two glasses. Drizzle over a little of the orange juice.

2 Hull and chop the strawberries, reserving two for decoration. Place a spoonful on top of the sponge fingers in each glass.

3 Mix together the fromage frais and sugar. Spoon half the mixture on top of the strawberries, dividing it between the two glasses.

4 Divide the remaining sponge fingers between the two glasses, followed by the remaining strawberries and the fromage frais mixture.

5 Decorate each glass with a whole strawberry and then chill for 20 minutes to 1 hour before serving.

Variation If you prefer, use 125 g (4½ oz) flavoured low fat yogurt – raspberry, strawberry or orange would work well – instead of the fromage frais and sugar, for 2½ **POINTS** values per serving.

Fruity Eton Mess

Enjoy the sharp–sweet flavours in this simple dessert.

Serves 4

zest from a lime
4 tablespoons lime juice
2 passion fruit
2 oranges
300 g (10½ oz) 0% fat Greek yogurt
200 g (7 oz) low fat soft cheese
1 teaspoon vanilla extract
artificial sweetener, to taste
sprigs of fresh mint or lavender, to decorate

---

2 *POINTS* values per serving
9 *POINTS* values per recipe

C **182 calories** per serving

Takes **10 minutes** to prepare

V

✱ not recommended

1 Put the lime zest and juice into a non metallic bowl. Scoop the seeds and pulp from the passion fruit into the bowl.

2 Using a sharp, serrated knife, remove the peel and pith from the oranges. Do this over the same bowl to catch the drips. Segment the oranges, removing all the membrane. Gently stir half the segments into the passion fruit mixture.

3 Mix together the yogurt and soft cheese with the vanilla extract. Add sweetener to taste.

4 Stir the two mixtures together loosely, then share between four serving glasses, adding the remaining orange segments as you layer the desserts. Spoon any juices on top. Chill until ready to serve, decorated with mint leaves or lavender sprigs.

Tip Try not to overmix the fruits with the yogurt mixture – it's meant to look messy.

Lemon Ice Cream

A creamy lemon ice cream to be savoured and enjoyed with friends on a hot summer's day.

Serves 6

450 ml (16 fl oz) low fat custard
150 g (5½ oz) lemon curd
200 g (7 oz) low fat natural yogurt
zest of a lemon

2½ POINTS values per serving
14 POINTS values per recipe

C **155 calories** per serving

Takes **10 minutes** + at least **4 hours** freezing

V

✱ recommended

1 Beat together the custard, lemon curd and yogurt, then stir in the lemon zest.

2 Pour the mixture into a plastic freezer proof container with a lid and place it in the freezer.

3 After 45 minutes take the container out of the freezer. Whisk the contents with a fork, breaking up the ice crystals and making sure to scrape the frozen mixture from the sides of the container.

4 Freeze for a further 45 minutes then whisk again. Repeat the whole process twice more and then leave to freeze for about 3 or 4 hours. Alternatively, pour into an ice cream maker and follow the manufacturer's instructions.

Crème Caramel

This perfectly simple, stylish dessert is a real winner. You'll see versions of it throughout Europe, and it's enjoyed everywhere.

Serves 2

40 g (1½ oz) granulated sugar
2 small eggs
½ teaspoon vanilla extract
2 teaspoons caster sugar
200 ml (7 fl oz) skimmed milk

 3 POINTS values per serving
6 POINTS values per recipe

C 210 calories per serving

Takes **10 minutes** to prepare,
45–50 minutes to cook

V

✱ not recommended

1 Preheat the oven to Gas Mark 2/150°C/fan oven 130°C.

2 Put the granulated sugar and 2 tablespoons of water into a heavy based, medium saucepan and heat gently to dissolve it. Do not stir. Turn up the heat and cook until the sugar begins to caramelise, turning a rich golden colour. Quickly divide this caramel between two ramekin dishes.

3 Break the eggs into a mixing bowl and beat in the vanilla extract and caster sugar. Pour the milk into the same pan used for the caramel and warm it a little, and then pour it over the egg mixture. Beat together, and then strain this mixture through a sieve into the dishes.

4 Put the dishes into a roasting pan or baking dish, and pour in enough warm water to come halfway up the sides of the dishes. Transfer to the oven and bake for 45–50 minutes until the crème caramels are set. Cool, and then serve them in the dishes, or run a knife around the edges and turn them out on to serving plates.

Jamaican Rum Pudding

This delicious version of trifle will go down a treat.

Serves 4

4 x 50 g (1¾ oz) slices of ready-made Jamaican Ginger cake
227 g can pineapple pieces in natural juice
1 small banana, sliced thinly
1 tablespoon rum
500 g carton low fat custard
150 g (5½ oz) 0% fat Greek yogurt
a pinch of ground cinnamon or ginger, to decorate

 5½ POINTS values per serving
22 POINTS values per recipe

C **363 calories** per serving

Takes **10 minutes** + **15 minutes** chilling

V

✱ not recommended

1 Arrange the ginger cake between four individual sundae dishes. Drain the pineapple, reserving the juice, and place the pineapple pieces in the dishes together with the banana slices.

2 Spoon the rum and reserved pineapple juice over the fruits. Spoon the custard on top, to cover completely.

3 Spoon the yogurt on top of the custard. Chill for 15 minutes to allow the sponge to soak up the juice. Lightly sprinkle with ground cinnamon or ginger. Serve.

Variation For special occasions, replace 3 tablespoons of pineapple juice with rum or brandy (in addition to the 1 tablespoon in the ingredients already), for an extra ½ **POINTS** value per serving.

Wonderful and Warming

A hot pudding or crumble – just what everyone fancies on a cold autumn or winter day. Try old favourites like Fruits of the Forest Steamed Pudding, a fresh Lemon and Passion Fruit Pudding, a fruity Autumn Crumble, or go for something unusual such as Spiced Carrot Puddings.

Hot puddings can be light and delicious – try these and see

Autumn Crumble

You can use fresh autumn fruit for this lovely crumble if it is in season, rather than frozen. Serve with 1 tablespoon low fat natural yogurt or low fat custard per person, for an additional ½ **POINTS** value per serving.

Serves 6

6 Bramley cooking apples, peeled, cored and chopped
250 g (9 oz) frozen forest fruits, defrosted
25 g (1 oz) caster sugar

For the crumble topping
40 g (1½ oz) demerara sugar
100 g (3½ oz) porridge oats
50 g (1¾ oz) plain flour
2 teaspoons ground ginger
50 g (1¾ oz) low fat spread

3½ **POINTS** values per serving
21½ **POINTS** values per recipe

C **231 calories** per serving

Takes **30 minutes** to prepare, **20 minutes** to cook

V

✳ recommended

1 Preheat the oven to Gas Mark 4/180°C/fan oven 160°C. Place the apples, forest fruits and sugar into a lidded saucepan with 2 tablespoons of water. Cover and cook for 20 minutes or until softened to a pulp. Keep an eye on the fruit and add a little more water if it starts to dry out.

2 Meanwhile, put all the ingredients for the crumble in a food processor and whizz until the mixture resembles fresh breadcrumbs.

3 Pour the stewed fruit into an ovenproof dish and scatter the crumble over the top. Bake for 20 minutes or until golden and bubbling.

Tips You can make the crumble in advance, up to the point where it goes in the oven. Keep it in the fridge, then pop it in the oven when you sit down to eat dinner.

If you don't have a food processor, mix the crumble topping together with your fingers.

Variation For a sweeter crumble, use six of any dessert apples in place of the Bramley apples. The **POINTS** values will remain the same.

Cherry Batter Pudding

This gorgeous hot pudding is easy to make – and so yummy to eat.

Serves 2

30 g (1¼ oz) plain flour
1 egg
100 ml (3½ fl oz) skimmed milk
½ teaspoon vanilla extract
2 teaspoons caster sugar
low fat cooking spray
125 g (4½ oz) fresh cherries, stoned
½ teaspoon icing sugar, for dusting

2½ *POINTS* values per serving
4½ *POINTS* values per recipe

164 calories per serving

Takes **10 minutes** to prepare,
25 minutes to cook

V

✱ not recommended

1 Preheat the oven to Gas Mark 6/200°C/fan oven 180°C.

2 In a bowl, whisk the flour, egg, milk, vanilla extract and sugar together to make a smooth batter.

3 Spray two individual, shallow, ovenproof baking dishes (or one larger one) with the cooking spray. Heat in the oven for 2–3 minutes.

4 Divide the cherries between the dishes, then pour in the batter. Quickly return the dishes to the oven and bake for 20–25 minutes, until risen and golden.

5 Sprinkle each pudding with the icing sugar and serve at once.

Tip Try not to open the oven door to check the puddings until 20 minutes has passed, otherwise the batter may not rise.

Crunchy Topped Rhubarb with Ginger

A variation on an old favourite, this modern rhubarb crumble is simply delicious.

Serves 4

450 g (1 lb) rhubarb, trimmed and cut into
  2.5 cm (1 inch) pieces
3 tablespoons reduced sugar strawberry jam
50 g (1¾ oz) caster sugar
juice of an orange
1 tablespoon cornflour

For the topping

75 g (2¾ oz) porridge oats
50 g (1¾ oz) fresh white breadcrumbs
25 g (1 oz) demerara sugar
4 tablespoons runny honey, warmed
½ teaspoon ground cinnamon
low fat cooking spray

5 POINTS values per serving
21 POINTS values per recipe

C   **290 calories** per serving

Takes **30 minutes** to prepare,
25 minutes to cook

V

✱   not recommended

1 Place the rhubarb in a pan with the strawberry jam, caster sugar and orange juice and cook gently until tender. Preheat the oven to Gas Mark 4/180°C/fan oven 160°C.

2 Mix the cornflour with 1 tablespoon of cold water to make a paste and stir into the rhubarb mixture. Cook until the juices thicken and then transfer to a shallow overproof dish.

3 In a bowl, mix together the oats, breadcrumbs, sugar, honey and cinnamon.

4 Scatter over the rhubarb and spray with the cooking spray. Bake for 20–25 minutes until the topping is crunchy.

Tip Sweeten the rhubarb with artificial sweetener instead of sugar if you want to save on **POINTS** values. Stir the sweetener in after you've stewed the rhubarb. You will save ½ a **POINTS** value per serving.

Baked Apple Custards

These comforting little cups of apple-flavoured egg custard are just the thing when you feel like a treat.

Serves 4

350 g (12 oz) cooking apples, peeled, cored and diced
1 tablespoon runny honey
25 g (1 oz) custard powder
300 ml (10 fl oz) skimmed milk
15 g (½ oz) artificial sweetener
1 egg, separated
a pinch of ground nutmeg

1½ POINTS values per serving
7 POINTS values per recipe

C **110 calories** per serving

Takes **20 minutes** to prepare,
25 minutes to cook

V

✻ not recommended

1 Preheat the oven to Gas Mark 2/150°C/fan oven 130°C.

2 Place the apples and honey in a small, lidded saucepan with 1 tablespoon of water. Cover and simmer gently for 5 minutes until the apples begin to soften.

3 Whisk the custard powder into the milk and heat gently in a separate saucepan until you have a smooth, thick custard. Remove the pan from the heat and beat in the sweetener, egg yolk and cooked apples.

4 In a clean, grease-free bowl, whisk the egg white until it forms stiff peaks, then fold it into the apple custard. Divide the mixture between four ramekin dishes. Sprinkle a little ground nutmeg over each one and bake for 25 minutes. Serve warm.

Tip If you don't have ramekin dishes, use heat resistant china cups instead.

Oaty Peach Crumble

This comforting crumble makes use of canned fruit so that you can prepare a hot pudding for the family, even when you are in a hurry.

Serves 4

2 x 411 g cans peach slices in natural juice
50 g (1¾ oz) low fat spread
100 g (3½ oz) wholemeal plain flour, sifted
25 g (1 oz) soft light brown sugar
2 tablespoons artificial sweetener
1 teaspoon ground cinnamon
75 g (2¾ oz) porridge oats

4½ **POINTS** values per serving
19 **POINTS** values per recipe

C **322 calories** per serving

Takes **10 minutes** to prepare,
25 minutes to cook

V

✱ not recommended

1 Preheat the oven to Gas Mark 4/180°C/ fan oven 160°C. Drain the juice from the peaches into a jug or bowl and set aside. Tip the peach slices into a baking dish and add 6 tablespoons of the juice.

2 In a mixing bowl, rub the low fat spread into the flour. Stir in the sugar, sweetener, cinnamon and porridge oats. Sprinkle in 2 tablespoons of peach juice and stir until the mixture just begins to form small clumps.

3 Scatter the crumble over the peaches and bake in the oven for 25 minutes until the topping is crisp and golden.

Marmalade Bread and Butter Puddings

Delicious individual bread and butter puddings with a sharp citrus tang. Just right to end a meal.

Serves 4

low fat cooking spray
75 g (2¾ oz) low calorie marmalade
40 g (1½ oz) low fat spread
6 slices Weight Watchers white bread
50 g (1¾ oz) sultanas or raisins
2 tablespoons artificial sweetener
zest of an orange
2 eggs
350 ml (12 fl oz) skimmed milk
15 g (½ oz) golden caster sugar

4 POINTS values per serving
15 POINTS values per recipe

270 calories per serving

Takes **10 minutes** to prepare, **40 minutes** to cook + **30 minutes** standing

V

✱ not recommended

1 Preheat the oven to Gas Mark 3/160°C/fan oven 140°C. Spray four 250 ml (9 fl oz) ramekins with the cooking spray. Using a fork, mash the marmalade with the low fat spread.

2 Spread the bread with the marmalade and spread mixture. Remove the crusts and cut the slices into small fingers.

3 Share out half the bread fingers, marmalade side up, between the ramekin dishes. Sprinkle with the sultanas or raisins, the sweetener and half of the orange zest. Top with the remaining bread fingers.

4 Beat the eggs into the milk and pour over the bread. Leave to stand for half an hour and then sprinkle with the sugar and the remaining orange zest.

5 Put the ramekins on a baking sheet. Bake in the oven for 35–40 minutes or until the puddings are set and the top is golden and puffed up. Serve immediately.

Crunchy Fruit Crumbles

Everybody loves a fruit crumble. These are made individually, preventing you from going back for a second helping.

Serves 4

200 g (7 oz) canned pear halves in fruit juice
60 g (2 oz) fresh raspberries
1 teaspoon treacle
2 teaspoons boiling water
60 g (2 oz) no added sugar muesli

1 *POINTS* value per serving
4½ *POINTS* values per recipe

C **80 calories** per serving

Takes **10 minutes** to prepare,
12 minutes to cook

V

＊ not recommended

1 Preheat the oven to Gas Mark 4/180°C/fan oven 160°C.

2 Drain the pears, reserving the juice, and dice the fruit. Divide the pears and raspberries between four ramekin dishes. Drizzle 1 tablespoon of the reserved juice over the top of each and discard the remaining juice.

3 Place the treacle in a small measuring jug and add the boiling water. Stir together.

4 Place the muesli in a bowl, pour over the treacle liquid and mix together well until all the muesli is coated.

5 Divide the muesli between the four ramekin dishes and place on top of the fruit. Place the dishes on a baking tray.

6 Cook in the oven for 10–12 minutes, until the crumbles are golden and bubbling.

7 Serve the crumbles warm or cold.

Variation Try 200 g (7 oz) canned mandarins with 60 g (2 oz) fresh peaches instead of the pears and raspberries. The *POINTS* values will remain the same.

Apple and Plum Puddings

Try this up-to-date version of a traditional British pudding – you'll love it.

Serves 4

50 g (1¾ oz) low fat spread
50 g (1¾ oz) golden caster sugar
2 dessert apples, peeled, cored and sliced thinly
2 plums, stoned and sliced
25 g (1 oz) raisins or sultanas
a pinch of ground mixed spice or cinnamon
3 x 45 g (1½ oz) slices from a thick cut, large white loaf, crusts removed
2 tablespoons elderflower cordial
4 tablespoons low fat natural yogurt, to serve

---

4 **POINTS** values per serving
16 **POINTS** values per recipe

C 232 **calories** per serving

Takes **15 minutes** to prepare,
30 minutes to cook

V

✳ recommended

1 Preheat the oven to Gas Mark 5/190°C/fan oven 170°C.

2 Melt the low fat spread in a large saucepan. Use a tiny amount to grease four individual pudding basins or ramekins.

3 Add the sugar, apples, plums, raisins or sultanas and mixed spice or cinnamon to the saucepan. Cut the bread into small cubes and add to the mixture. Make up the elderflower cordial to 150 ml (5 fl oz) with cold water and add to the mixture, tossing to combine.

4 Pack the mixture into the prepared dishes. Stand the dishes on a baking sheet. Bake for 25–30 minutes, until golden brown. Cool for a few minutes. Turn them out and serve each pudding with a tablespoon of yogurt.

Variation Use 150 ml (5 fl oz) unsweetened orange juice instead of the elderflower cordial, if you'd rather. The **POINTS** values will remain the same.

Fruits of the Forest Steamed Pudding

A scone crust reduces the **POINTS** values of this steamed dessert.

Serves 6

225 g (8 oz) self raising flour
1 teaspoon baking powder
110 g (4 oz) low fat spread
50 g (1¾ oz) golden caster sugar
150 ml (5 fl oz) skimmed milk
500 g bag frozen forest fruits, defrosted

 4 POINTS values per serving
25 POINTS values per recipe

C **269 calories** per serving

⏱ Takes **25 minutes** to prepare,
1 hour 20 minutes to steam

V

✱ not recommended

1 Sift the flour and baking powder into a bowl. Add the low fat spread and rub in with your fingertips until the mixture resembles breadcrumbs.

2 Stir in a tablespoon of the sugar and then mix to a dough with the milk. Reserving a third of the mixture, line an 850 ml (1½ pint) heatproof basin with the dough.

3 Mix 300 g (10½ oz) of the fruit with the remaining sugar. Spoon into the basin. Place the remaining dough on top, spreading to reach the sides. It will be thin, but will rise on cooking.

4 To steam, cover with a lid or folded piece of baking parchment, secured with string. Bring a large pan of water to the boil, and place the pudding in a steamer on top. The water level should be below the steamer. Steam for 1 hour 20 minutes until risen and dry on the top. Check during cooking to ensure the pan doesn't boil dry.

5 Meanwhile, place the remaining fruit in a saucepan with 3 tablespoons of water and simmer for 3–4 minutes. Remove from the heat and push through a nylon sieve to form a sauce. Discard the pips.

6 Remove the pudding from the steamer, carefully loosen the sides with a knife and invert on to a serving plate. Serve with the sauce.

Pear Tart with Cinnamon Topping

A surprise custard base and a sweet crunchy topping turn this pear tart into something really special.

Serves 6

low fat cooking spray
4 x 15 g sheets filo pastry
250 g (9 oz) low fat ready-made custard
2 x 410 g cans pear halves in natural juice,
  drained
50 g (1¾ oz) porridge oats
1 teaspoon ground cinnamon
1 teaspoon maple syrup

---

2 POINTS values per serving
11½ POINTS values per recipe

C **116 calories** per serving

Takes **10 minutes** to prepare,
20 minutes to cook

V

✳ not recommended

1 Preheat the oven to Gas Mark 4/180°C/fan oven 160°C.

2 Spray an 18 cm (7 inch) cake or flan tin with the cooking spray. Line the tin with a sheet of the filo pastry and spray again with the cooking spray. Place another pastry sheet on top of the first but at a slightly different angle, so that the corners stick up. Spray again and repeat with the other two sheets of pastry so that the tin is lined. Put the tin in the oven for 2–3 minutes until slightly golden.

3 Arrange the pears, cut side down, on the tart base and pour the custard over.

4 In a small bowl, mix together the oats, cinnamon and maple syrup. Scatter this over the tart and spray again with the cooking spray. Bake for 20 minutes or until golden brown and crispy.

Tip Keep the filo pastry under a damp tea towel as you make the tart so it doesn't dry up.

Pineapple Upside-down Cake

A traditional pudding, this deserves to be popular again. Try it and see.

Serves 6

low fat cooking spray
2 tablespoons golden syrup
225 g (8 oz) can pineapple rings in juice,
   drained and juice reserved
4–5 glacé cherries, halved
100 g (3½ oz) low fat spread
50 g (1¾ oz) soft brown sugar
2 eggs, beaten
175 g (6 oz) self raising flour
1 teaspoon cornflour

4½ *POINTS* values per serving
26 *POINTS* values per recipe

C 275 calories per serving

Takes **25 minutes** to prepare,
45 minutes to cook

V

✳ not recommended

1 Preheat the oven to Gas Mark 4/180°C/fan oven 160°C and spray an 18 cm (7 inch) round cake tin with the cooking spray.

2 Heat the golden syrup gently in a pan until runny, then pour into the base of the tin. Arrange the pineapple rings on top and place half a glacé cherry in the centre of each ring, cut side up.

3 Cream together the low fat spread and sugar until pale and fluffy then add the eggs a little at a time, beating between each addition.

4 Fold in the flour and enough of the reserved pineapple juice to give a dropping consistency. Spoon on top of the pineapple rings and bake for 45 minutes or until risen, golden and firm to the touch.

5 Meanwhile, mix a tablespoon of the remaining pineapple juice with the teaspoon of cornflour. Put the rest of the juice in a pan and heat. Stir in the cornflour and bring to the boil, stirring, until the sauce thickens. Turn the pudding out on to a serving plate and serve with the hot pineapple sauce.

Variation Upside-down puddings can be made in the same way using canned pears or fresh cooking apples, peeled and cored and thinly sliced. The *POINTS* values per serving will remain the same.

Ginger Puddings

These lovely little ginger puddings are just the thing to warm you up on a cold day.

Serves 4

low fat cooking spray
80 g (3 oz) self raising flour
1 teaspoon ground ginger
¼ teaspoon ground cinnamon
¼ teaspoon baking powder
¼ teaspoon bicarbonate of soda
40 g (1½ oz) soft brown sugar
1 egg, beaten
8 teaspoons corn oil
2 teaspoons golden syrup

 4 POINTS values per serving
15½ POINTS values per recipe

C **224 calories** per serving

🕐 Takes **10 minutes** to prepare,
30 minutes to cook + **5 minutes** cooling

V

✱ recommended

1 Preheat the oven to Gas Mark 5/190°C/fan oven 170°C. Spray four 150 ml (5 fl oz) pudding basins (tins, glass or foil) with the cooking spray.

2 Sift all the dry ingredients, except the brown sugar, into a bowl. Add the brown sugar, then whisk in the rest of the ingredients.

3 Divide the mixture between the prepared pudding basins and place them on a baking tray. Bake in the oven for 25–30 minutes, until firm to the touch.

4 Cool in the basins for 5 minutes before loosening with a knife and turning out on to serving plates.

Spiced Carrot Puddings

These individual puds are a little like passion cake with a spiced carrot mixture.

Serves 4

low fat cooking spray
1 small orange
110 g (4 oz) carrots, grated finely
2 eggs, beaten
250 g tub Quark
1 teaspoon mixed spice
4 teaspoons artificial sweetener

 1½ POINTS values per serving
5½ POINTS values per recipe

C   108 calories per serving

Takes **10 minutes** to prepare,
20 minutes to bake + **5 minutes** cooling

V

✳   not recommended

1 Preheat the oven to Gas Mark 4/180°C/fan oven 160°C. Lightly coat four ovenproof ramekins or pudding basins with the cooking spray.

2 Finely grate the zest from the orange, then slice the orange thinly, removing the pith. Place an orange slice on the base of each ramekin or pudding basin. Mix the remaining ingredients with the orange zest and spoon into the ramekins over the orange slices.

3 Place the ramekins in a small roasting tin and then fill the roasting tin with sufficient hot water to come two thirds of the way up the sides of the pots. Bake in the oven for 20 minutes until set. They should only just be turning brown on top.

4 Remove from the roasting tin and leave to cool for 5 minutes in the ramekins before loosening the sides with a knife and turning out to serve.

Sticky Banana Toffee Puddings

A delicious sticky and filling pudding.

Serves 4

50 g (1¾ oz) low fat spread
50 g (1¾ oz) light muscovado sugar
1 large egg, beaten
1 teaspoon vanilla extract
50 g (1¾ oz) self raising white flour
½ teaspoon ground ginger
1 banana, mashed
25 g (1 oz) dates, chopped
1 tablespoon skimmed milk
2 tablespoons golden syrup
2 x 150 g pots low fat custard, to serve

4½ POINTS values per serving
19 POINTS values per recipe

C **345 calories** per serving

Takes **15 minutes** to prepare,
30 minutes to cook

V

✳ recommended

1 Preheat the oven to Gas Mark 4/180°C/fan oven 160°C. Use a tiny amount of the low fat spread to grease four individual pudding basins or ramekin dishes.

2 Cream the remaining low fat spread and sugar together until light and fluffy. Gradually beat in the egg and then stir in the vanilla extract. Sift in the flour and ground ginger, and fold them in with a large metal spoon.

3 Stir the banana into the creamed mixture with the dates and milk.

4 Put half a tablespoon of golden syrup in each pudding basin or ramekin. Divide the creamed mixture between the pudding basins or ramekins and level the surface of each. Stand the basins or dishes in a roasting pan and pour in enough warm water to come halfway up their sides.

5 Bake for 25–30 minutes until risen and golden. Cool for a few moments while you heat the custard. Run a knife around each pudding and turn out into dishes. Serve at once, with the custard.

Variation Use raisins or sultanas instead of the dates. The **POINTS** values will be 5 per serving.

Lemon and Passion Fruit Pudding

This zingy pudding is so simple to make and absolutely delicious.

Serves 4

low fat cooking spray
50 g (1¾ oz) low fat spread
75 g (2¾ oz) caster sugar
2 eggs, separated
finely grated zest and juice of a large lemon
50 g (1¾ oz) self raising flour, sifted
250 ml (9 fl oz) skimmed milk
2 passion fruit, halved

3½ **POINTS** values per serving
14 **POINTS** values per recipe

C 231 calories per serving

Takes **10 minutes** to prepare,
30 minutes to cook

V

* not recommended

1 Preheat the oven to Gas Mark 4/180°C/fan oven 160°C. Spray a baking dish, measuring about 15 x 20 cm (6 x 8 inches), with the cooking spray.

2 In a bowl, beat the low fat spread, sugar, egg yolks and lemon zest together for 1 minute until pale. Whisk in the flour, followed by the lemon juice and then the milk to give a thin batter.

3 In a separate, clean, grease-free bowl, whisk the egg whites until they form stiff peaks. Gently fold the egg whites into the batter, then pour the foamy mixture into the baking dish. Spoon the passion fruit seeds randomly over the pudding.

4 Bake on the centre shelf for 30 minutes until golden brown and firm in the centre.

Apricot Clafouti

A calfouti is a traditional French dish made by baking fruit in a batter. This one uses fresh apricots.

Serves 4

low fat cooking spray
6 small apricots, stoned and each one sliced into
    6 pieces
50 g (1¾ oz) plain flour
50 g (1¾ oz) caster sugar
2 eggs
200 ml (7 fl oz) skimmed milk
1 teaspoon vanilla extract

2½ *POINTS* values per serving
9½ *POINTS* values per recipe

C **169 calories** per serving

Takes **10 minutes** to prepare,
25 minutes to cook

V

✱ not recommended

1 Preheat the oven to Gas Mark 6/200°C/fan oven 180°C. Spray four shallow ovenproof dishes approximately 12 cm (4½ inches) wide with the cooking spray.

2 Place the slices from one and a half apricots (9 slices) in a circle in each one of the dishes.

3 Beat all the remaining ingredients together in a large bowl and share out the mixture between the dishes.

4 Bake in the oven for 20–25 minutes, or until golden and the top springs back when gently pressed. Serve immediately.

Tip Cherries are traditional in clafouti. If they're in season, use 300 g (10½ oz) stoned fresh cherries instead of the apricots. The *POINTS* values per serving will remain the same.

Peach and Blueberry Cobbler

Peaches and blueberries are a wonderful combination and this cobbler is a great way to show them off.

Serves 4

225 g (8 oz) self raising flour, plus 1 tablespoon for dusting
½ teaspoon ground cinnamon
50 g (1¾ oz) low fat spread
25 g (1 oz) fruit sugar (fructose)
1 teaspoon skimmed milk

For the filling
400 g (14 oz) canned peach halves in natural juice
150 g (5½ oz) fresh or frozen blueberries
1 tablespoon cornflour

5½ POINTS values per serving
22 POINTS values per recipe

C **345 calories** per serving

Takes **20 minutes** to prepare, **25 minutes** to cook

V

✱ not recommended

1 Sift the flour and cinnamon into a mixing bowl and rub in the low fat spread with your fingertips until the mixture resembles fine breadcrumbs. Stir in the fruit sugar and then add enough cold water to mix to a soft dough.

2 Drain the peaches, reserving the juice, and chop roughly. Toss with the blueberries. Heat the reserved juice in a small pan until it boils. Mix the cornflour with a little cold water and stir into the hot liquid. Cook, stirring, until thickened and then pour over the fruit and toss well.

3 Spoon the fruit into a shallow ovenproof dish and set aside. Preheat the oven to Gas Mark 5/190°C/fan oven 170°C.

4 Roll out the cobbler mix on a lightly floured surface to about 1 cm (½ inch) thick. Stamp out eight rounds using a 5 cm (2 inch) pastry cutter and arrange around the edge of the dish. Brush the cobblers with a little milk and bake for 20–25 minutes, until well risen and golden. Serve warm or cold.

Tip Make individual portions in small ramekins. Divide the cobbler mixture into four large rounds and place on top of each one.

Fruit and Nut Baked Apples

A simple dessert for two – this is a great way to use up cooking apples.

Serves 2

2 cooking apples
25 g (1 oz) raisins
1 tablespoon flaked almonds
2 teaspoons maple syrup
a pinch of ground cinnamon
1 teaspoon low fat spread

2½ POINTS values per serving
5 POINTS values per recipe

C **145 calories** per serving

Takes **10 minutes** to prepare,
25 minutes to cook

V

✱ not recommended

1 Preheat the oven to Gas Mark 5/190°C/fan oven 170°C. Line a roasting tin with baking parchment.

2 Wash the apples well and remove the centre core. Score the skin around the middle with a sharp knife. Arrange in the tin.

3 Mix together the raisins, almonds, maple syrup and cinnamon and pack equal amounts into each apple. Dot the top of each with a little low fat spread and bake for 20–25 minutes, until the apples are soft and pulpy. Serve warm.

Index